INVEST IN LIVING

HOME~MADE PICKLES AND CHUTNEYS

by

BABS HONEY

EP Publishing Limited
1978

The *Invest in Living* Series

All About Herbs
Gardening under Protection
Getting the Best from Fish
Getting the Best from Meat
Home-Baked Breads and Scones
Home Decorating
Home Electrical Repairs
Home Goat Keeping
Home Honey Production
Home-made Butter, Cheese and Yoghurt
Home Maintenance and Outdoor Repairs
Home Poultry Keeping
Home Rabbit Keeping
Home Vegetable Production
Home Woodworking
Meat Preserving at Home
Unusual Vegetables
101 Wild Plants for the Kitchen
Wild Fruits and Nuts

About the Author

Babs Honey and her husband live in Wales; the surplus produce from Dick's farming is used by Babs to make pickles and chutneys. When members of their large family come to visit, the pickles and chutneys are eaten enthusiastically with home-made bread and cheese as a midday snack.

Babs Honey has also written *Home-Baked Breads and Scones* in this series.

Acknowledgements

The author would like to thank Messrs. Sarsons Vinegars, the Fishguard Fruit Company Limited, Mrs Joan Lloyd of Treglemais Fach, Mrs Jean Platt, and John Hughes. Her husband Dick has been especially helpful with growing the produce and then preparing it. Babs Honey would also like to thank her daughter-in-law, Nancy, who spurred her into collecting chutney recipes.

Contents

Note on Metrication

Many of the recipes in this book are hundreds of years old and have been adapted by successive generations to round imperial measures of pints, ounces and so on. Rather than distort these amounts by converting them to metric measure in the recipes themselves (and also to avoid cluttering the recipes with figures of both standards) we give here tables showing equivalents which can be used when necessary.

oz	g		lb	kg		pints		litres
$\frac{1}{4}$	7		1	0.5		$\frac{1}{4}$ (5 fl oz)		0.1 (142 ml)
$\frac{1}{2}$	14		2	0.9		$\frac{1}{2}$ (10 fl oz)		0.3 (284 ml)
$\frac{3}{4}$	21		3	1.4		$\frac{3}{4}$ (15 fl oz)		0.4 (426 ml)
1	28		4	1.8		1 (20 fl oz)		0.6 (568 ml)
2	57		5	2.3		2		1.1
3	85		6	2.7		3		1.7
4	113		7	3.2		4		2.3
5	142		8	3.6		5		2.8
6	170		9	4.1		6		3.4
7	198		10	4.5		7		4.0
8	227					8 (1 gallon)		4.6
9	255							
10	283					1000 millilitres (ml) = 1 litre (l)		
11	312							
12	340							
13	369							
14	397							
15	425							
16	454							

1000 grammes (g) = 1 kilogram (kg)

Introduction

A little of what you fancy does you good
A Victorian song associated with
Marie Lloyd

Gardening has come back into fashion to such an extent that not only is there always a waiting list for allotments in cities and large urban areas, but many elderly people and others with over-large gardens are splitting them up for enthusiasts to take over. Even city dwellers with just a window-box cleverly placed are growing tomatoes, herbs, and lettuces. Since some crops only too often mature all at once, producing a glut, there is sure to be a percentage of fruit and vegetables surplus to requirement. Naturally, freezers can take up much of this over-production, but not everyone owns a freezer and in any case there is a limit to their capacity.

If you don't have the space or inclination to produce any food yourself, there is a chance these days that somewhere within your reach there is a farm, market garden or private producer who will gladly supply large quantities of what you require. You may be able to pick-and-pay, which makes for a pleasurable day out in the country as well as for economy.

Even if none of the above seems to apply to you, there are still seasonal gluts to take advantage of; all fruit and vegetables can be bought much more cheaply at some times of the year than at others, and pickles and chutneys are a way of enjoying them all year round.

This is where the old-fashioned recipes come into their own, because in spite of phenomenal changes in our way of life compared with even a decade ago, people's palates change very little. The speed with which pots of home-made chutneys, pickles, etc. are bought up from the Women's Institute market stalls and other country produce shops is a sure indication that our modern way of eating still has room for a spot of relish in the diet.

Despite all the 'convenience' foods, people are, it seems, wanting some of the traditional additions to basic dishes to make them even more attractive and appetising. Maybe it is because of convenience foods that some palates have suddenly gone on hunger-strike against any more of this sophisticated form of feeding. On the other hand, should it be that you are committed through force of circumstances to using convenience foods, then a taste of home-made chutney, pickle or ketchup could be a very welcome stimulant to the appetite.

Naturally, home-produced foods are by definition fresher and therefore more nourishing. They also have more taste-appeal to the average eater, retaining as they do, more of the vitamins desirable for good health and full vigour—to which we are all by grace entitled.

So, in spite of, or because of, the modern way of preparing meals, a call has gone up for a return to good fresh food prepared in the home kitchen, involving more than ever the skills and talents of men, women and children. Perhaps one of the most interesting and heart-warming developments in present-day trends, is the fact that more and more women are happily and thankfully delegating some of the creative cooking to children and male members of the family, realising at last, as part of their emancipation, that not only can others perform the tasks long regarded as 'women's work', but can perform them with great skill, imagination and enjoyment.

Finally, there are two well-intentioned

warnings for those who wish to take up this rewarding hobby:

The first is that you may have to keep a tight rein on yourself to prevent pickling from becoming a compulsive occupation —after all, there is a limit to the number of jars of pickled onions, for example, that you can store under the bed!

Secondly, before getting into this thing too deeply, do remember that not everyone enjoys the smell of boiling vinegar about the house! So please make allowances and be prepared for any lack of enthusiasm or encouragement on the part of the rest of the household when you embark on this fascinating pastime.

Good pickling!

Equipment, Ingredients and Method

Give us the tools and we will finish the job
Winston Churchill, 1941

Equipment

One of the nicest things about making pickles is that you are quite likely to have the equipment already in your kitchen, but before we go any further, two points must be brought to your notice.

1. Important—never use copper, brass or iron for cooking with vinegar

The reason for this is that the chemical action of the vinegar on copper, brass or iron is highly dangerous. When using enamel, make sure it is not cracked, otherwise the vinegar will work its way through and lift the enamel off the metal base. Iron saucepans, so basic a utensil in olden days, ruin pickles by turning them black and giving them a bitter flavour.

2. Never use glazed crocks for pickles, etc.

The action of the vinegar on the glaze produces a mineral poison.

Jars

Since glazed crocks must never be used with vinegar, glass jars are the obvious choice. This also, of course, has great advantages in that the pickle can be identified through the glass even if the label has dropped off through damp, or worn off through age.

Obviously they must be sparkling clean, but if you use one of those much-advertised washing-up liquids to achieve this result, it is advisable to have a bowl of clear water to rinse the jars after washing, as nothing tastes worse than soapy chutney or pickles. To avoid cracking the jars, they must be warm, if not hot, to receive the hot contents. A very low oven is useful for this as it also has the effect of sterilising the jars. However, if this is not available, simply leave the hot water in the jars until the last possible minute, tip out the water and shake a little, then fill the jar (a few drops of boiled water are not going to spoil the chutney).

JARS

CAPS & LIDS

LABELS

Jar Caps or Lids

If metal caps are used, they should be lined with waxed cardboard discs, or two sheets of waxed paper (the paper from cereal packets will do) to stop the vinegar coming into contact with the metal. This will avoid corrosion. Clarified mutton-fat painted on paper may be used as a protective layer between a metal lid and the vinegar to prevent corrosion and evaporation. Nowadays, many metal lids have a plastic coating and therefore may be safely used to cover pickles.

Special lids may be obtained through the Women's Institute if you are a member. Plastic lids are quite suitable. If you use corks, cover them with waxed paper or sheets of greaseproof paper to prevent them from touching the vinegar as they carry mould.

Failing all else, cover the jars with waxed paper followed by two thicknesses of cotton painted with melted wax and tied tightly; this is not, however, as satisfactory as a well-fitting screw-on lid.

Knife

A knife is needed for preparing the vegetables and fruit; it should be of stainless steel, if you wish to avoid having stained fingers. Apples, especially, are best done with a stainless steel knife. This is no problem, since most cooking knives are in any case made of stainless steel.

Labels

Stick-on or self-adhesive labels are invaluable, but failing all else, Sellotape and ordinary paper may be used. Always label your jars—you may think at the time of bottling that you'll remember what they contain, but a year later it may be a different story.

Ladle

Enamel, stainless steel, china or plastic ladles are all equally suitable for dishing up the chutney into the jars. Plastic is perhaps most useful as it does not hold the heat.

Saucepans

Most modern saucepans are suitable for making chutneys—stainless steel, uncracked enamel, aluminium, etc.—but, as mentioned above, **not copper, brass or iron pans.**

Sieve

Avoid using tin or other cheap metal sieves; only nylon, hair or stainless steel sieves must be used, as cheap metals discolour the chutney.

Spoons

Use only a wooden or heat-resistant plastic spoon for stirring the pickle. A long-handled wooden spoon is of course desirable, otherwise you will be fishing about for it in the hot chutney at frequent intervals, because chutney in particular requires repeated stirring on account of its density and sweetness. Any other type of spoon tends to discolour the mixture and can leave a bitter taste.

A teaspoon, a dessertspoon and a tablespoon for measuring are also needed. If no scales are available, the following tip may be useful: 1 heaped tablespoon or 2 rounded dessertspoons of sugar weigh near enough 1 oz.

Teacup

An unbreakable plastic cup is sometimes more useful than a ladle for transferring your chutney into the hot jars, because unless the jars have very wide mouths it can be a tricky operation.

Ingredients

Salt

Salt is a natural preservative, along with sugar and vinegar, but in chutneys and pickles its main feature is to extract the surplus water found in fruit and vegetables. For example, cauliflower, marrow, cucumber, cabbage and tomato contain over 90 per cent water. This tends to be related to the season; for instance, in a dry summer the water content is naturally slightly lower. Water can be extracted by 'brining' (see p. 20) or, in the case of chutneys, by longer boiling. It is a question of choice as to which method you adopt.

Spices

Of all the ingredients in pickles and chutneys, spices above all need treating with respect. The best idea is first to make a small quantity of the recipe (reducing everything pro rata) in order to test your reaction to the chosen spices. Since spices are entirely for flavouring, i.e. they will not affect the consistency of the chutney, be bold and make your own choice. Naturally, the ideal is to buy separate spices and mix them to taste, but many people nowadays are too busy to indulge in this, so ready-spiced vinegar may be used.

Allspice (pimento) is a very useful berry, since it seems to give a pleasant mixture of many flavours.

Where the recipe reads chillies, cayenne pepper may be substituted, since this is produced by grinding chillies.

If you have time, it makes interesting reading to delve into the origins of the various spices.

Sugar

For most purposes, ordinary granulated sugar will do, but some recipes are improved by using soft brown sugar. You will notice in some recipes that parentheses have been put round (brown) sugar—this is to indicate that either may be used. Golden syrup may equally well be used—this was frequently a substitute in the rationing times during and after World War II. Castor sugar is more expensive and no benefit will be derived from using it. Some of the recipes may be on the sweet side for many modern palates; do not hesitate to cut down the sugar and/or dried fruit to suit individual tastes.

Vinegar

This is the basic ingredient of all pickles and chutneys. In fact, the success of your efforts depends on the quality of your vinegar. In these days, it is no problem to buy good vinegar and it may be obtained in gallon containers from most supermarkets, while many grocers carry quart bottles. There are various kinds of vinegar, and the country of origin determines its nature. For instance, white wine vinegar comes mainly from the wine-producing countries of France and Germany, whereas malt and spirit vinegars come from beer-producing countries such as Britain. Scotland, of course, produces distilled vinegar because of her whisky distilleries, and you can't do better than that!

However, the most useful and popular vinegars are of malt and spirit and these are also the best because they have the best flavour and are wholly reliable. Wine vinegar may be used, but it is rather extravagant since the delicate flavour is wasted in pickles. Bottled vinegar is perhaps the safest to use, since it has a slightly higher acetic acid strength, but it must be pointed out that draught is usually cheaper.

Fruit

Naturally, summer is the busy time for picking the fruit—it must be done then and there, if the crop is not to be wasted. But if you have a freezer, only the gathering need be done at the height of the season, since most fruits will deep-freeze success-fully. Some of the chutney- and pickle-making can therefore be postponed to a less busy period, since the fruit comes out of the freezer in as good condition as it went in. Simply freeze the fruit on trays, then pack. It's not much use planning the freezing operation in military style since

the whole success of using the fruit season to the full lies in seizing oppor-tunities as and when they appear. Many a crop of, for instance, raspberries, has been saved from thieving birds by the expedient of nipping out with a jam-jar at frequent intervals.

Apples

Many gardens are blessed with established apple trees planted many years ago, and there are very few varieties of cooking apple which are unsuitable for chutneys and pickles. Windfalls are a natural choice for using up in this way. Peeling apples is a

matter of choice. Many of us cannot bear to waste the peels, however, and overcome the unpleasantness of lumps of skin by chopping the fruit up small or mincing it. Apple is a very good mixer—it blends with most fruits.

Apricots

These can be used fresh or dried, though many of us regard them as a luxury. However, as a special Christmas or birthday present for someone who has everything, a jar of this most acceptable relish could solve a problem.

Blackberries

One of the few fruits we have for free, the gathering of which affords a day out in the country. The only disadvantage is the number of pips, but these can either be accepted (if no dental plate is involved!) or they can be sieved out for more particular palates. Of all fruits, resist the temptation to wash blackberries, since this makes them mushy and somewhat tasteless. The cooking of them will immediately destroy any germs.

Bilberries

The bilberry is another free fruit if you are fortunate enough to live near a source of supply. These vitamin-rich berries are tedious to gather, but are quick to cook and make a change.

Bananas

Some greengrocers are only too pleased to sell over-ripe bananas at a give-away price. Unless absolutely rotten, most of the flesh may be used, and makes a delicious chutney.

Cherries

Sweet pickled cherries are a luxury. Make the most of them, if you have them, by making this delicate pickle.

Crab-apples

Anyone knowing of a good crab-apple tree could substitute these wild fruits for apples; the work involved may be overcome by simply putting the apples, roughly cut, into a saucepan, covering with water and reducing them to a pulp, stirring carefully and frequently. This pulp may then be sieved and used like any other fruit, with added sugar for those with a sweet tooth.

They can also be kept whole for pickling.

Cranberries

Not a plentiful fruit in this country, but when obtainable a delicious chutney may be made to serve with cold turkey or game.

Currants, black, red or white

These are not much used in relishes, but spiced currants make a change from ordinary pickles.

Damsons

Not a common plum, but their distinctive flavour makes another delicious chutney or pickle to serve with cold meat.

Elderberries

The Botary Bush, as the Yorkshire folk call it, was once allowed to grow by every self-respecting gardener, and many superstititions were attached to this useful

tree. The fruit provides a helpful source of Vitamin C, and was once used extensively to relieve coughs and colds. Many wide open spaces contain elderberry trees growing wild.

Figs

Very few gardens have a fig tree, but dried figs are used in chutney-making to give a very special flavour.

Gooseberries

A delicious chutney may be made very easily from gooseberries, and they may also be pickled whole.

Lemons

At certain times of the year, lemons may be bought at a very reasonable price. The pickle or chutney made from lemons has a very distinctive and interesting flavour.

Oranges

With their unique flavour, oranges may be incorporated in delicious chutneys, and make a delectable pickle, especially good served with cheese.

Greengages

Although their season is short and they are not grown profusely, greengages have a beautiful golden colour. Watch out for them in August, around St Bartholomew's day, the 24th. My sixth son, Sam, was born on 23 August, the day after an orgy of greengage eating!

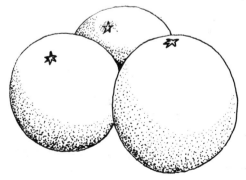

Peaches

Peaches, like apricots, fall into the luxury class, but fresh or dried peaches may be used to make unusual and delicate relishes.

Pears

Not as adaptable as apples, but a useful fruit, especially mixed with other fruits and vegetables.

Plums

Plums do not keep for very long and therefore may be bought from orchards at a reasonable price.

Quinces

Well-established old gardens sometimes contain a quince tree, and in this era of adventurous gardening, more people will have access to quinces (a japonica-type fruit) than ever before. Some Women's Institute country markets sell quinces.

Raisins, Sultanas and Currants

Some people consider that a chutney without sultanas is not a chutney. Their addition makes very little difference to the consistency, so it is entirely a matter of choice. They add a sweetness to the flavour, so extra sugar may be added to replace them. They also add 'texture' to the chutney, and prevent the mixture from becoming too bland and sauce-like.

Raspberries

Raspberry vinegar at one time was served especially to pregnant women and teenage girls, but as a winter drink it is a great comfort to anyone engulfed in a heavy cold. Drink it hot in bed!

Rhubarb

The poor man's friend. However small the garden, a crown of rhubarb may be usefully grown, and there are many ways of using one's ingenuity to concoct ways of 'forcing' it.

Tomatoes

Probably the best known of all ingredients for chutneys and pickles. The green ones are best, though ripe ones also make a very good chutney. Tomatoes are a good 'mixer', and may be used with most things.

Vegetables

Beans

See French Beans or Runner Beans.

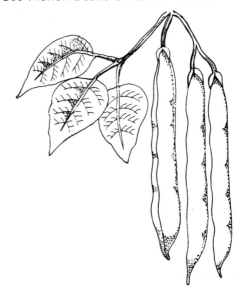

Beetroot

Delicious pickles and chutneys may be made from beetroot. They are naturally sweet and add a richness to life.

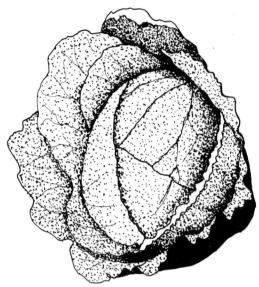

Cabbage, red

Pickled red cabbage is a great favourite with many people, and very simple to make—the cabbages are easily grown, too.

Cabbage, green

Look for green cabbage in Australian Chow-Chow and other recipes.

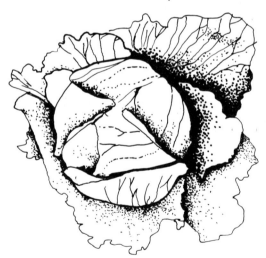

Carrots

A good 'mixer' but not too exciting on their own, carrots are really only used for colour.

Cucumber

Small young cucumbers, not yet ripe, may be pickled whole. Sliced, mature cucumbers mix well with other pickle ingredients.

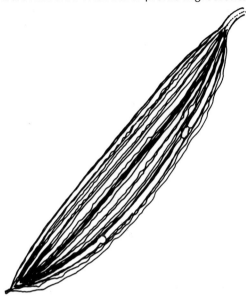

Celeriac

A comparatively new vegetable, but being grown by enterprising gardeners, celeriac makes a delicious pickle.

French Beans

An easily-grown vegetable, but with a comparatively short season; the only bean which can be pickled. French beans may also be used in mixed pickles and chow-chows.

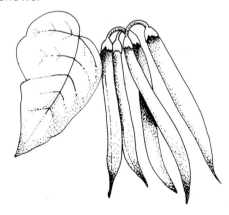

Celery

This plant needs constant watering but makes an excellent addition to chow-chow and other mixed pickles.

Garlic

You either love or hate the distinctive taste of garlic. Some people use wild garlic when it is in season, but onion may be used instead of raw garlic or cloves of garlic. See Onions and Shallots.

Horseradish

In many gardens horseradish is considered a weed, but if you only have a little plant, do as Uncle Fred does—take the root out, use as much as is required, and then stick it back in the soil. Good roast beef doesn't need it—overcooked roast beef is improved by it.

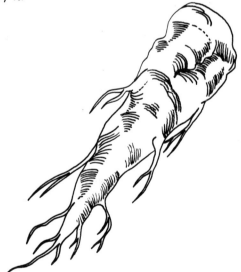

Marrow

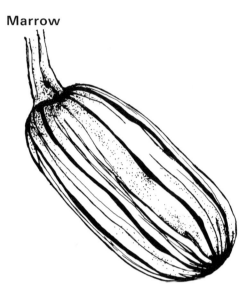

Marrow is perhaps one of the most useful fruits you can grow in your garden, if you are interested in jam, chutney or pickle making. It has very little food value, being largely composed of water, but it has the virtue of fitting in with many other fruits and vegetables and is thus very adaptable, as well as providing bulk. Marrows may even be used for making a sort of rum!

Mushrooms

Since the advent of grow-it-yourself mushrooms, they can no longer be regarded as a luxury. Those fortunate people able to pick them for free may care to pickle a few.

Shallots

Strictly speaking, shallots are a herb, but they may be used like onions or garlic since in flavour they come midway between the two. Shallots are easily grown, since one bulb yields six or seven more.

Onions

Many people consider a day without an onion is a day wasted. They seem to be compulsive eating for some, and are the most useful tasty vegetable par excellence. But if you are anti-onion, leave them out altogether or substitute chives. See Garlic and Shallots.

Turnips

An easy vegetable to grow or buy. Turnips are first cousin to the mangold/mangel-wurzel.

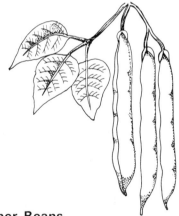

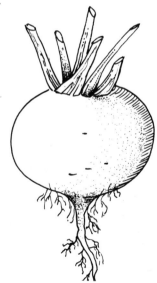

Runner Beans

A most prolific producer in good years. They deep-freeze easily, blanched or unblanched, providing they have been sliced, and may then be taken out and used at your convenience.

Miscellaneous

Mint

Mint sauce is such a popular accompaniment to lamb that it has many addicts. However, mint also makes a delicious cooked or uncooked chutney.

Nasturtiums

The pickled seeds make a good substitute for capers. They may also be added to mixed pickles for a change of flavouring. Nasturtiums are prolific growers and the seed is easily pickled; a useful addition to any larder.

Preserved Ginger

A recipe for making 'mock' preserved or crystallised ginger can be found on p. 22, and it will be a useful ingredient in other recipes. The main function of the 'ginger', as well as to add sweetness and flavour, is the same as that of sultanas—to add texture and 'bite' to an otherwise smooth chutney.

Samphire

Samphire grows on cliffs around our seashores; gathering it used to be a seashore trade—a 'dreadful trade', as Shakespeare says, since it was so dangerous. However, a good pickle may be made for those brave souls who know where and how to gather the weed.

Walnuts

Pickled walnuts are an acquired taste; either you like them or you don't. The nuts must be gathered at exactly the right moment when the shell is still green and soft but the fruit is formed. This is usually early in July.

Method

Preparation of Vegetables

Only tender vegetables, freshly picked, should be used. Leave small vegetables, such as nasturtium seeds, small onions and baby cucumbers, whole.

■ **Golden Rule 1:** Never pick today and leave the pickling till next week. Although we don't want the water in vegetables, neither do we want shrivelled second-rate ingredients. Therefore, make sure you've got time to complete the operation before you start it.

■ **Golden Rule 2:** Unless you are a compulsive washer, or the vegetables are earthy or have been sprayed within the last week or so, try to restrain yourself from washing them. Most vegetables are clean enough anyway, and it only adds more water.

Brining

The object of brining is to draw the water and carbohydrates from the vegetables and at the same time to prevent bacteria from growing. Dry-brine watery vegetables such as marrow, cucumber, etc. and wet-brine the crisp ones, e.g. cabbage, cauliflower. For pickles, rinse all vegetables well under a cold tap to get rid of the brine before draining and drying and packing into jars with vinegar, pepper and spices.

To Dry-Brine: For cucumbers, marrows, tomatoes and other watery vegetables allow a good $\frac{1}{2}$ oz of salt to 1 lb of prepared vegetables. Arrange the prepared vegetables in layers, sprinkling salt between each layer. Cover and leave to stand for 12 hours.

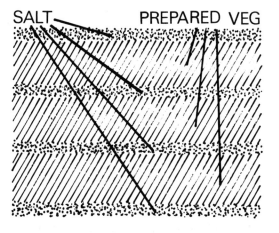

SALT   PREPARED VEG

To Wet-Brine: For cauliflower sprigs, etc. allow 4 oz salt to 2 pints of water. This is sufficient to prepare 2 lb crisp vegetables. Dissolve the salt in the water, place the vegetables in a bowl, and cover them with the brine. Leave to stand for 12 hours. Onions are better brined for two days. Beetroot are prepared for pickling by simply cooking in salted water until tender.

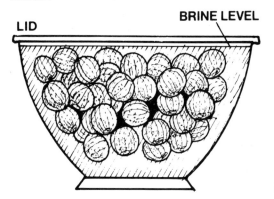

LID   BRINE LEVEL

■ **Golden Rule 3:** To prepare beetroot for *boiling*, put one hand between the beetroot and the top of the leaves, and with the other hand twist off the top of the leaves—this prevents 'bleeding'. Throughout their preparation treat beetroot very tenderly, merely brushing off the dirt carefully with the fingers before boiling. Too much handling causes bleeding.

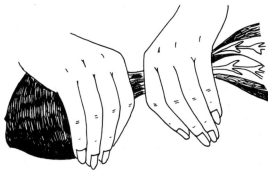

■ **Golden Rule 4:** It is better to keep beetroot and cauliflower apart—they do not make good bedfellows.

Spices

When using 'mixed pickling spice' it is customary to tie the spices in the corner of a muslin bag or a piece of an old clean sheet and suspend the pouch by string from the saucepan handle into the chutney. This mixed pickling spice will usually contain pieces of whole red and black peppers, pimento, ginger, cloves and mace. For convenience, ground spices may be used. Ready-spiced vinegar may also be used for pickles.

Vinegar

■ **Golden Rule 5:** When the vinegar has been poured onto the pickles, make sure it covers the vegetables with at least $\frac{1}{2}$ in. to spare because vinegar tends to evaporate, and any vegetables left high and dry soon become unpalatable-looking and unpleasant in colour.

Once the vinegar has been poured on, slip a palette or long-handled knife down the side of the jar to encourage the bubbles of air to rise and disperse and then cover down as tightly as possible with a suitable vinegar-proof lid. **Never allow vinegar to come in contact with metal lids.**

Fruits and sweet vegetables must be gently cooked in a syrup of vinegar and sugar in order for the syrup to penetrate the fruit.

■ **Golden Rule 6:** Never boil the vinegar for sweet pickles, only heat through.

■ **Golden Rule 7:** For crisp, firm pickles cold vinegar only should be used— nothing is worse than a soggy pickled onion.

Note on Quantities

You can estimate roughly the quantity of pickle or chutney produced by each recipe by adding up the total weight of the ingredients, allowing $1\frac{1}{4}$ lb per pint of vinegar. Naturally, the quantities can then be adjusted to suit your needs, as long as you take care to keep the proportions correct.

Poor Man's Preserved Ginger or Mock Crystallised Ginger

You will find this recipe very useful for adding to other pickle and chutney recipes.

1 vegetable marrow
Sugar
Ground ginger

Peel the marrow, remove the seeds, cut it into 1 in. cubes and weigh it. Put the cubes into a preserving pan or large heavy saucepan, cover with water, and add 1 lb sugar and 1 oz ground ginger for each 1 lb of marrow. Boil very gently until the cubes become transparent, but do not allow them to break up. Remove them from the pan and drain, retaining the juice.

Make a syrup by boiling together $\frac{1}{2}$ pint of the juice from the preserving pan, 2 oz ground ginger and 1 lb granulated (or preserving) sugar. Put the pieces of marrow carefully into jars, and when the syrup is quite thick, fill up the jars with it. Cover closely.

Pickles and Relishes

The imaginary relish is so sweet that
it enchants my sense
From 'Troilus and Cressida' by
Shakespeare

Once men had discovered how to make wine, there is no doubt that women soon learned to use the sour wine or vinegar (the failures?) for preserving foodstuffs. The prospect of pickling and preserving vegetables, fruits and herbs may be quite new to us, but the Ancient Greeks and Romans were hard at it in their day, using mostly long round vases with wide mouths. They took great pride and joy in their pickles, using oil, brine, vinegar, and infinite time and patience. They even managed to pickle meat and fish, which must have been a great advantage in those very pre-freezer days.

Even in Britain pickles add greatly to our winter diet. Many a dull cold dinner on a pre-war washday-Monday was en- livened by a bit of tasty chutney or pickle even for the poorest of the poor. Modern slimmers, who are so numerous, may care to make any of the following recipes substituting saccharin tablets for sugar, the result being a tasty variation in what can become in some cases a dull diet.

The beauty of pickling is that in nearly every month of the year something is available to be pickled. Also, so many of the fruit and vegetables that are easy to grow are perfect for pickling.

Here then are a selection of recipes given to me by many friends and collected over the years. You will soon discover that making pickles is an easy and pleasant pastime and most rewarding. Not only does it add that certain something to a cold dish, but you will feel an extra pride in being able to select one colourful jar of pickles from among the many varieties visible on your shelves.

Apple Pickle (1)

1 lb cooking apples
8 oz onions (large)
1 pint white vinegar
1 tbsp salt
A few chillies
½ oz whole peppers

Peel and cut up the apples and onions and pack them in a jar with the chillies. Boil the vinegar, salt and peppers, and pour it over the fruit in the jar.

When cool, cover closely.

Apple Pickle (2)

6 lb good cooking apples (e.g. Bramleys seedlings)
3 pints vinegar
12 shallots
12 oz sugar
1 oz turmeric
½ oz ground ginger
½ oz mustard
12 peppercorns
12 cloves

Peel the apples, cut them into $\frac{3}{4}$ in cubes, spread them on a dish and strew with a little salt. Leave to stand for 24 hours and then drain. Tie the cloves and peppercorns in a piece of muslin or cotton and place them and all the other ingredients, apart from the apples, in a saucepan. Boil for 10 minutes, remove the muslin bag, then add the strained apple chunks and cook for 15 minutes or until tender, without smashing.

Bottle, keeping the chunks of apple as whole as possible, and tie down when cool.

August Pickle

Here is an economical mixed pickle with the added flavour and colour of carrots. Carrots on their own are not very interesting —but in this recipe they add to the attractiveness of the pickle in the jar.

1 lb carrots, sliced
$\frac{1}{2}$ lb runner beans, cut in 1 in slices
3-4 oz (or less) onion, chopped
$\frac{1}{2}$ pint vinegar—to start with
1 tsp salt
$\frac{1}{4}$ tsp turmeric
Optional: 4 oz sugar
            black pepper
            paprika

Mix all the ingredients together in a saucepan. Add sugar, if liked, and stir until dissolved, over a slow heat. Add black pepper and paprika to taste. Boil until clear and thick, stirring frequently. Add more vinegar now, if needed.

Seal at once in hot jars.

Beetroot Pickle

$1\frac{1}{2}$ lb beetroot
2 pints vinegar
$\frac{1}{2}$ oz allspice
$\frac{1}{2}$ oz peppercorns
1 tbsp salt if liked

Bring the vinegar, allspice, peppercorns and salt to the boil in a covered enamel pan, and leave to cool, tightly covered, for two hours. If liked, add 1 tablespoonful of salt to the vinegar.

Wash the beets, being careful not to break the skins. Place in boiling water and simmer for $1\frac{1}{2}$–$2\frac{1}{2}$ hours according to the size of the beets.

When cool, remove the skins and slice the beet thinly—$\frac{1}{8}$ in is good for storing. Pack into bottles and cover completely with the spiced vinegar.

Beet Relish

1 lb cooked beetroot, chopped fine
1 lb raw cabbage, chopped
1 cupful freshly-grated horseradish
1 tbsp mustard
1 pint vinegar
8 oz sugar
A pinch of cayenne
1 tsp salt
1 saltspoon white pepper

Mix the ingredients together well and cook for 30 minutes. Put into jars and cover closely. Add more vinegar if necessary.

This relish is very good served with fish.

Note. If you want to store this pickle for long, don't pack the beetroot too tightly but cover it well and seal thoroughly to exclude air.

Steep the blackberries and ginger in the vinegar for 12 hours. Strain off the vinegar and keep the blackberries and ginger on one side. Bring the vinegar to the boil. Add the berries and sugar and boil for 30 minutes. When cold, add the spice. Mix well, put into jars and cover.

Sweet Beetroot Relish

A useful, attractive and easily made pickle which can be used all year round.

1 packet of raspberry jelly
1 pint boiling vinegar
1½ lb cooked beetroot

Melt the packet of jelly in the hot vinegar and add the sliced beetroot. Fill the jars with the beetroot and jelly and leave to set.
Cover tightly.

Blackberry Pickle

5-6 lb blackberries
1 pint white vinegar
2 lb sugar
1½ oz allspice
½ oz ground ginger

Pickled Carrots

Equal-sized carrots
Vinegar

Wash the carrots and boil them in salted water until tender. Drain them, then peel and cut into thin slices. Pack the slices tightly in jars or bottles, and fill with vinegar. Cover closely.

Pickled Celeriac

From Czechoslovakia, keeps well.

1 celeriac
1 large onion
Salt
A little ginger
Vinegar
Water

Clean the celeriac and cut it into thick slices. Slice the onion. Put alternate layers of onion and celeriac into suitable jars. Sprinkle each layer with salt and ginger— easy does it!

Cover the vegetables with vinegar and water (4 parts vinegar to 1 part water) and seal securely.

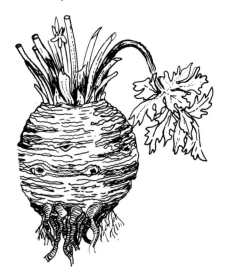

Cherry Pickle

An uncooked pickle, delicious and distinctly different. Ready after one month.

Ripe red cherries
Sugar to taste
A little cinnamon, mace and nutmeg, tied into several small cherry-sized muslin bags
Vinegar

Stone the cherries and place them in a jar alternately with layers of sugar. In every other row of fruit place one of the bags containing cinnamon, mace and nutmeg.

Fill the jar with cold vinegar when the cherries, etc. come three quarters of the way up the jar. Cover securely.

Pickled Cherries (1)

Cherries
Vinegar
Sugar

Remove all speckled cherries; put the good ones in a jar and pour over them hot vinegar and sugar in the proportions of 8 oz sugar per pint of vinegar, making sure that all the fruit is covered.

Leave to stand for one week. Pour off the vinegar, then boil and skim it and pour it while still hot over the fruit again.

As soon as it is cold, tie down securely.

Pickled Cherries (2)

2 lb stoned cherries
1 lb sugar
½ tsp allspice
A little mace and cinnamon
½ pint vinegar

Place the cherries in layers in a saucepan, with the sugar and spices sprinkled over each layer. Add the vinegar and boil for 5 minutes. Take out the fruit and pack into hot jars; let the syrup boil until thick and then strain it over the fruit. Seal the jars tightly with fitting lids.

This recipe may be used for pickling plums, damsons or any other stoned fruit.

Chow-Chow

Pickle addicts are so crazy about this concoction that I give here two slightly varying recipes, one from a new American friend and one from an old Australian Edwardian recipe book given to me years ago.

Australian Chow-Chow

4 lb green tomatoes
2 lb string beans
1 lb small white onions
4 tbsps white mustard seed
4 oz green or red peppers (mixed)
2 large cabbage heads
1 lb brown sugar
Salt
Vinegar
4 oz mustard
2 oz cloves
2 oz celery seed
2 oz allspice
1 oz turmeric

Slice the tomatoes, sprinkle lightly with salt, leave overnight. Next day, pour off the brine.

Chop the cabbage, onions and beans; chop the tomatoes separately, and mix with the spices. Put all the ingredients in a saucepan and cover with vinegar. Boil for 3 hours.

American Chow-Chow

3 large cucumbers
3–4 green tomatoes
1½ lb string beans (scarlet runners)
24 small onions
1 large cauliflower
24 or more small pickled gherkins
Brine
Mustard sauce:
4 oz plain flour
½ pint mild cider vinegar
1½ tbsps turmeric
6 tbsp dry mustard
4 pints malt cider vinegar
3 tbsps celery seed
2 lb brown sugar

Remove the cucumber peel if it is tough, and slice them. Cover with brine made in the proportion of 1½ cups salt to 1 gallon water, and leave for 12 hours. Meanwhile, slice and keep separately green tomatoes and string beans (Scarlet Runners), which have now been well drained. Peel and slice the onions, break into small sprigs one large cauliflower, and slice the pickled gherkins. Keep these last three ingredients separate and pour boiling water over them. Bring to boiling point and drain well.

Now combine all the vegetables.

Then make the mustard sauce; mix and stir the flour, mild cider vinegar, turmeric and dry mustard until smooth.

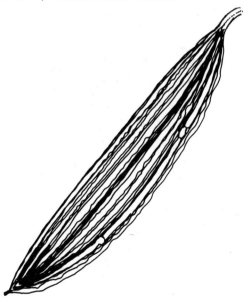

Bring just to the boil the malt cider vinegar, sugar and celery seed; slowly add the flour mixture, stirring constantly. When the sauce is smooth and boiling pour it over the mixed, drained vegetables; add salt to taste. Bottle the pickles in very clean jars and seal securely.

Chillies Pickled in Sherry

Given to me by an American working in the UK.

Long red chillies
Sherry

Make sure the chillies are quite clean, then pack them into a few nice-looking jars with really well-fitting lids (plastic not metal) and cover them with sherry (which can be the cheap-and-cheerful kind). Seal the bottles or jars and store away from sight until you remember them!

Both the peppers and the sherry can be used in cooking as a delicious and different form of flavouring. Just keep on topping up the sherry and the chillies as you use them and the pickle will keep for years.

Spiced Crab Apples

One of the for-free fruits. Enjoy your day out carefully picking the crab apples (remembering next year's crop and other folk), then come home and make this delicious and different pickle.

5 lb crab apples gathered in late
   summer, washed but not peeled
2½ lb sugar
2 pints spiced vinegar
Ground ginger to taste (optional)

Wipe the crab apples with a damp cloth and remove the stalks. Boil the sugar and

vinegar together, then pop in the apples and simmer till tender, but take care not to overdo them or they will start to fall apart. Dish them up carefully from the vinegar and pack whole into hot jars. Boil the syrup again until it becomes thick, then fill up the jars.
   Seal securely.

To pickle Young Cucumbers

An early Victorian recipe, just for fun.

Choose nice young gherkins, spread them on dishes, salt them and let them lie for a week. Drain them, put them in a jar, pour boiling vinegar over them. Set them near the fire, covered with plenty of vine leaves; if they do not become a tolerable good green pour the vinegar into another jar, set it over the hot hearth, and when it boils pour it over them again, covering with fresh leaves; and do this until they are as good a colour as you would wish; but as it is now known that the very fine green pickles are made so by using brass or bell-metal vessels which, when vinegar is put into them, become highly poisonous, few people like to eat them.

Sliced Cucumber and Onion Pickle

Cucumbers ⎱ in equal proportions
Onions ⎰ or according to taste
A little pepper
A little ground ginger
Vinegar

Cut the cucumbers and onions into slices, quite thickly, and sprinkle with salt. Next day drain them in a colander and leave them draining for 5 or 6 hours. Then put them in a stone jar (or similar because of the boiling hot vinegar) and cover with boiling vinegar. Keep them in a warm place; put a lid or plate on top. Leave for 20 minutes, drain off the vinegar, bring it to the boil and pour it over the cucumbers and onions again. Cover again right away. Keep on in this way until the cucumbers are green; the last time add the pepper and ginger to the vinegar before pouring it over the onions and cucumbers.

Tie or seal down well in small stone or glass jars.

Slimmers' or Diabetics' Pickled Cucumbers, sometimes called Saccharin (Uncooked) Pickle

1 gallon cider vinegar
1 tsp liquid saccharin (or equivalent in tablets)
3 tbsps mixed spices
1 tbsp powdered alum
2 tbsps dry mustard
1 oz salt
16 cupsful small cucumbers

Wash and dry the cucumbers and pack them in sterilised jars. (The jars can be sterilised by bringing them to the boil in a saucepan which has been filled with cold water, or by heating them in an oven, either by residual heat, after having cooked or by turning the oven on very low and leaving the jars at this temperature for an hour.)

Mix together the remaining ingredients, without heating them, and pour the mixture over the cucumbers. Seal and store in a dark place.

Sweet and Sour Spiced Cucumber Pickles

A very tasty and delicious pickle.

10 lb very small cucumbers (ridge or outdoor will do very well)
Brine made from 1 cup coarse salt and 6 pints water (make half quantity first and double up if necessary)
Vinegar mixture:
4 pints cider vinegar
11 cups sugar
2 oz whole mixed spice
1 oz stick cinnamon
1 tsp cloves
4 tbsps lime water

Soak the cucumbers for 24 hours in the brine. Remove them, cover with boiling water, drain quickly in a colander and pack closely while hot in sterilised jars. Cover at once with the vinegar mixture just at boiling point.

Seal the jars at once, very securely for storing.

Spiced Currants

1 lb blackcurrants
12 oz brown sugar
$\frac{1}{4}$ tsp salt
A pinch each of ground cloves, nutmeg and allspice
$\frac{1}{2}$ teacup brown malt vinegar
1 tsp ground ginger
1 tsp ground cinnamon

Put the sugar, vinegar and spices into a saucepan. Bring slowly to the boil and then simmer gently for 5 minutes. Leave to cool.

Add the currants, and boil all together for a further 25 minutes.

Bottle in hot jars and seal well.

Pickled Damsons

1 lb damsons
$\frac{1}{2}$ pint vinegar
1 lb brown sugar
1 stick of cinnamon
1 tsp cloves

Prick the skins of the damsons with a steel needle and put them in a large jar. Boil together the vinegar, sugar and spices (tied in a muslin bag), then pour it over the damsons and leave it all to soak for 24 hours. Turn the whole mixture into a suitable saucepan and boil together for 5 minutes. Remove the spice bag from the pickle. Place in jars and seal when cold.

Damsons or Pears Pickled

8 lb damsons or cooking pears
4 lb sugar
2 pints vinegar
$\frac{1}{2}$ oz whole cloves
$\frac{1}{2}$ oz allspice
$\frac{1}{4}$ oz root ginger
$\frac{1}{4}$ oz stick cinnamon
Rind of half a lemon or 1 tsp citric acid

Wash and stalk the damsons; peel and core the pears and cut them into eighths or quarters according to size. Dissolve the sugar in the vinegar and add the spices, crushed and tied loosely in a muslin bag. Simmer the fruit in the spiced, sweetened vinegar until quite tender; then drain the liquid from the fruit, and pack the latter into jars, as neatly as possible. Boil the vinegar gently until slightly thick, and fill each jar with enough hot vinegar syrup to cover the fruit, then tie down and seal securely.

This pickle is better if kept some months before being used.

These fruits may also be pickled in unsweetened spiced vinegar. The ingredients and method of pickling are as above, omitting the sugar.

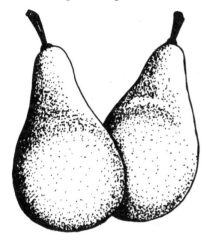

Pickled Dates

2 lb cooking dates
1 pint vinegar
Salt
1 tsp allspice
½ oz cinnamon

Stone the dates, halve them and pack into jars.

Boil the vinegar, salt, spice and cinnamon, then pour it over the dates to fill the jars.

Leave to cool, then cover.

Pickled Dried Fruit

Dried fruit is very easy to make into a delicious pickle since half the work has already been done. The water having been extracted, the pickling process is that much quicker.

1 lb dried fruit—apples, apricots, pears or peaches
2 lb sugar
3 pints ready-spiced vinegar

Place the dried fruit on flattish dishes or meat plates and soak it in the vinegar until nicely plumped up—say 48 hours—adding more vinegar overnight. Then pour off the vinegar into a saucepan and bring it to the boil with the sugar. Add the dried fruit and simmer gently until tender.

Remove the fruit carefully from the pickle and arrange in clean hot jars. Boil the liquor again until it is fairly thick and quite syrupy. Fill up the jars with the liquor and seal securely immediately. The pickle will keep for months if properly sealed but leave at least one week before sampling.

Pickled Eggs

16 eggs—about one week old
2 pints vinegar—white vinegar is
  best
1 oz peppercorns
½ oz ground ginger

Boil the eggs for at least 12 minutes, bang each egg against the table to loosen the shell, then steep all the eggs in cold water and leave for about half an hour. When the eggs are quite cold, shell them.

Put the vinegar and spices into a saucepan, bring to the boil and simmer for 10 minutes. While still boiling hot pour over the eggs until the latter are covered; when quite cold cork or cover jars most securely in order to keep airtight.

Will be ready for use in a month. These eggs are delicious eaten with celery salt.

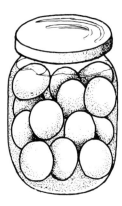

Elderberry Pickle

1 lb elderberries
2 tbsps sugar *or* 1 tbsp syrup
1 small onion
½ tsp ground ginger
½ tsp ground mixed spice
½ pint vinegar
A pinch of salt

Wash the berries and remove the stalks. Mash thoroughly.

Put all the ingredients into a suitable pan and bring to the boil.

Cook slowly till thick, stirring so that the mixture does not burn.

Bottle while hot in hot jars and tie down securely.

Fig Pickle

1 lb dried cooking figs
1 lb brown sugar
1 tsp allspice
1 tsp ground mace
½ pint vinegar
2 tsps ground cloves
2 tsps ground cinnamon

Wash the figs and leave them to soak for 6–8 hours in a bowl, just covering them with water. Then drain them in a colander.

Prepare the pickling liquor by boiling the sugar and vinegar until thick, then

add the remaining ingredients. Simmer for a few minutes before adding the figs. Cook gently for 1 hour.

Bottle and cover well.

Note: *This pickle is ideal to serve with cold boiled bacon, ham, poultry, pork or indeed any cold meat.*

Pickled French Beans (1)

Young French beans
Vinegar

Do not string the beans but put them whole into a strong salt and water solution till they become yellow, then drain off the liquid and wipe them dry.

Place them in an enamel pan or jar near heat, pour boiling vinegar over them and cover loosely. Renew the boiling vinegar every 24 hours (using the same vinegar strained off and re-boiled) until the beans become green again.

Then pour into jars, cover well and keep until required.

Pickled French Beans (2)

French beans are a useful fill-in until the scarlet runners come into season, but in some years the latter overtake the earlier beans, and so one is left with many French beans to use up. Here then is a second recipe which is spiced and sweet.

French beans
Vinegar
Salt
Pepper
2 tbsps brown sugar per pint of vinegar
1 tsp allspice per pint of vinegar

String the beans and slice them thinly. Boil them in water with a little salt until tender. Drain them in a colander, put them

in an enamel pan with enough vinegar to cover, add the salt, sugar and allspice and boil all together for five minutes.

Pour into bottles and cover while hot.

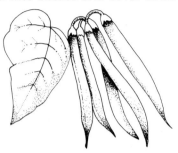

Pickled Gherkins, 1945 version

Gherkins
Brine made from 1 lb salt per gallon of water
Spiced vinegar

Place the gherkins in the brine and leave for 3 days. Drain well and pack into jars.

Pour hot, spiced vinegar over them, cover tightly and leave for another 24 hours in a warm place. Drain off the vinegar, boil it up, pour it over the gherkins again, cover tightly and leave for a further 24 hours; repeat this process until the gherkins are a good green colour. After the final process, a little more vinegar should be added if necessary, and the jars corked and stored.

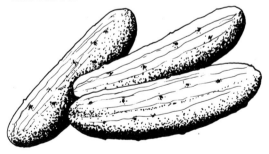

Gooseberry Pickle

3 lb gooseberries
1¼ lb sugar
¼ oz ground cloves
½ pint vinegar

Top and tail the gooseberries.

Put the fruit and all other ingredients into an enamel pan and boil until the mixture has the same consistency as jam, being careful to keep stirring all the time.

Put into hot jam jars and cover tightly when cold.

Pickled Greengages

2½ lb greengages
1 pint vinegar
1 lb sugar
1 oz cinnamon stick
½ oz whole cloves
½ oz allspice (pickling spice)
1 oz blade mace
Sultanas (optional)

Method 1. Wipe the fruit with a damp cloth if necessary. Prick several times with a darning needle and place in a large bowl. Warm the sugar and vinegar together. Place the spices in a muslin or cotton bag and tie on to the saucepan handle, then suspend the spice bag in the liquid and bring to the boil. Pour the hot liquor over the fruit, cover and leave to stand for 12

hours, leaving the spice bag soaking with the fruit.

Then drain off the syrup into the pan and bring to the boil again. Remove the spice bag. Pack the greengages into jars previously heated (otherwise the jars will crack) and seal securely right away—the sooner the better. There should be 2½ pints of pickle.

Method 2. For speed and if you have a lot of greengages, you may care to try the following way.

Dissolve the sugar in the vinegar and add the spices, tied up in a muslin bag. Add the fruit and some sultanas if liked. Boil until tender. Put into jars and seal right away.

Pickled Horseradish (1)

2 roots horseradish
2 cups vinegar
1 tsp salt

Scrub the horseradish roots in hot water until quite clean; scrape off the skin.

In a glass or stainless steel bowl mix the vinegar and salt.

Grate or mince the horseradish and pack into clean jars, layer by layer, pouring vinegar over each completed layer.

Cover well and seal securely. Store in a cool place and use within a fortnight.

Pickled Horseradish (2)

1 root horseradish
1 very small onion
2 cups vinegar

Scrape the horseradish and cut up the onion. Boil the vinegar and add the horseradish and onion.

Put them in a jar and leave for one week. Pour off the vinegar and boil it up again, then pour it over the horseradish.

Seal well.

Hot Pickle

4 lb green tomatoes
2 lb apples
4 large onions
Salt
1 lb brown sugar
4 pints vinegar
8 oz raisins
2 oz mustard seed
$\frac{1}{2}$ tsp cayenne
$\frac{1}{4}$ oz ground ginger

Slice the tomatoes, apples and onions, sprinkle with salt and leave overnight. Add the other ingredients, put them all in a suitable pan and boil very gently until soft. Pour into hot jars, tie down and seal well.

Pickled Indian Maize

Usually made in June.

3 green corn cobs
$\frac{1}{2}$ oz pickling spices
A few bay leaves
$\frac{3}{4}$ lb shallots
Salt
Vinegar
$\frac{1}{4}$ oz mustard seed

Place the green corn cobs in some well-salted cold water and bring to the boil. Remove the cobs and put them to drain.

Meanwhile, boil the vinegar and allow it to get cold.

When drained, put the cobs and shallots (peeled) in the jars with the spices, etc. and pour over the cold vinegar. Put in a good sprinkling of mustard seed and tie down very securely.

Indian Pickle

A useful, spicy pickle, started early in the season, which may be added to as surplus produce becomes available. This recipe makes a large amount of pickle, but it may be decreased to suit individual requirements. Take care to keep the proportions correct.

To each gallon of vinegar allow:

6 cloves garlic
2 oz black peppercorns
12 shallots
2 sticks horseradish (sliced)
$\frac{1}{4}$ lb bruised ginger
1 oz allspice
12 cloves
$\frac{1}{4}$ oz cayenne pepper
Ground pepper to taste
2 oz mustard seed
4 oz mustard
1 oz turmeric
Hard white cabbage
Cauliflower
Radish
French beans
Gherkins
Young ridge cucumbers
Small round pickling onions
Nasturtiums
Capsicums
Chillies, etc.

Cut the cabbage into slices, and the cauliflowers into small branches; sprinkle salt over them and let them stand for 2 days. Drain them and let them get dry before putting them into a very large jar, with garlic, shallots, horseradish, ginger, pepper, allspice and cloves in the above proportions. Boil sufficient vinegar to cover them, then pour it over them and when cold cover up to keep from dust.

As the other ingredients to be added to the pickle ripen, simply add them when they are ready, remembering however to wash them in a little cold vinegar first. Then make sure that they are **covered** by vinegar. If more vinegar should be needed, make sure that it is boiled before being added, when cold, to the rest. When you have collected all the things that you require, turn it all out into a large pan and mix thoroughly.

Now put the mixed vegetables into smaller jars without any of the vinegar. Boil the vinegar again, adding as much as will be required to fill the different jars and also cayenne pepper, mustard seed, turmeric and mustard, which must be well mixed with a little cold vinegar, allowing the quantities given above to a gallon of vinegar. Pour the boiling vinegar over the pickle and when cold, tie down **very** securely. If the pickle is required for immediate use, the vinegar should be boiled twice more, but the better way is to make it during one season to be eaten in the next.

Indian pickle will keep for years if care is taken to check regularly that the vegetables are quite covered by the vinegar.

Indian Relish

12 green tomatoes
12 cooking apples, peeled and cored
3 onions, peeled
5 cups vinegar
5 cups sugar
1 tsp red pepper
3 tsps ginger
1 tsp turmeric
1 tsp salt

Mince or chop finely the tomatoes, apples and onions. Boil together all the other ingredients. Now add the chopped ingredients and simmer for 30 minutes.

Pack the relish into hot jars and seal very securely.

Instant Pickle

An excellent old recipe.

Cucumbers	in whatever
Cooking apples	proportions
Onions,	you
medium-sized	like

$1\frac{1}{2}$ tsp salt
$\frac{3}{4}$ tsp cayenne pepper
1 wineglass soy sauce
1 wineglass sherry

Slice sufficient cucumbers, apples and onions to fill a 1 pint stone or glass jar, taking care to make the slices very thin.

Arrange them in alternate layers, shaking in salt and cayenne as you go. Pour on the soy sauce and sherry, then fill up with vinegar.

This pickle will be ready for use the day it is made.

Ladies' Delight Pickle

8 oz onions
8 oz apples
2 oz chillies
1 pint white wine vinegar
1 tbsp salt

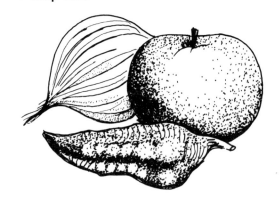

Chop the onions, apples and chillies. Boil the vinegar and salt and pour them over the other ingredients. Mix well and when quite cold put into small, decorative (if possible) jars.

This pickle tastes delicious with cold meats.

Pickled Lemons—Peeled

6 lemons—or more
Vinegar
To each quart (2 pints) of vinegar:
$\frac{1}{2}$ oz cloves
$\frac{1}{2}$ oz white pepper
1 oz bruised ginger
$\frac{1}{4}$ oz mace
$\frac{1}{4}$ oz chillies
1 oz mustard seed
$\frac{1}{2}$ stick horseradish, sliced
A few cloves of garlic

Peel the lemons and in each one make three slits, taking care that the slits are not so deep as to cut right through the lemons. Rub salt generously into each cut, then place the lemons in a dish for a week, turning them every other day. Dry them out most thoroughly, in the sun, or on a radiator, or in the residual heat of an electric oven, until the salt is perfectly dry.

Arrange them in a jar or jars, and pour over them sufficient boiling vinegar, to which all the other ingredients have been added in the relevant proportions, to cover the lemons completely. Tie down securely.

In about 9 months the lemons will be fit to use.

Pickled Lemons—Unpeeled

6 lemons
Brine
Vinegar
To each quart of vinegar:
$\frac{1}{2}$ oz cloves
$\frac{1}{2}$ oz white pepper
1 oz bruised ginger
$\frac{1}{4}$ oz mace
$\frac{1}{4}$ oz chillies
1 oz mustard seed
$\frac{1}{2}$ stick horseradish, sliced
A few cloves of garlic

Prepare a brine salty enough to support a new-laid egg in its shell. Soak the lemons in it for 6 days, stirring every day.

Boil 4 pints of water, drop the lemons in, and boil for 15 minutes. Then take them out, drain them and dry them by leaving them in a cloth until perfectly dry and quite cold.

Boil up sufficient vinegar to cover the lemons, having added the other ingredients in the relevant proportions.

Pack the lemons in a jar or jars, pour over the vinegar mixture, boiling hot, and tie down very securely.

The lemons will be ready for use in 12 months or rather less.

Pickled Mushrooms

1 lb young or button mushrooms
2 blades mace
$\frac{1}{2}$ tsp white pepper
Vinegar
1 tsp salt

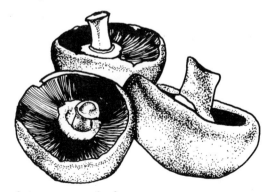

1 tsp ground ginger
A little chopped onion (about $\frac{1}{4}$ of an onion)

Remove and discard the mushroom stalks and wipe the mushrooms with a clean cloth. Put them into a pan or casserole with sufficient vinegar to cover and add the other ingredients.

Cook slowly with a well-fitting lid on the pan until the mushrooms have shrunk, then ladle them into hot jars and cover with the hot vinegar.

Tie down securely at once.

Here is a good sensible recipe for those who enjoy a mixed, traditional pickle.

Mustard Pickle

2 lb prepared marrow, cubed
2 lb mixed vegetables—
   cauliflowers, broken into sprigs
   runner beans, sliced
   ridge cucumbers, whole if small,
     sliced if larger
1 lb shallots, sliced

Pickle:
2 oz dry mustard
1 oz curry powder
½ oz turmeric
3 pints vinegar
1 tbsp plain flour
3 tbsps sugar
1 dstsp salt

Place the prepared vegetables on a large flat dish; sprinkle with a little salt. Next day, drain them and make the pickle by mixing all the dry ingredients together with sufficient of the vinegar to make a smooth paste. Pour the rest of the vinegar into a saucepan, then stir in the paste mixture. Cook carefully until thick, stirring frequently. While still hot, pour this over the prepared, drained vegetables and leave to stand for 24 hours, covered well. Then pack into sterilised jars and seal securely.

Another way is to cook the vegetables in the pickle for a good 3 minutes, then bottle and seal as before.

Pickled Onions

Onions are probably the best known and most popular pickle. There are many ways of producing a jarful of crisp pickled onions— here are just two of them. The first I call 'Dick's easy way'.

Sufficient onions to fill 2 jars
1 jar pure malt vinegar, ready spiced
1 tbsp sugar
1 tbsp salt
Mixed pickling spices (optional)

Method 1. Peel the onions under water or after scalding them in boiling water; this is for peeling-without-tears, and pack them into clean jars up to the necks. Sprinkle on the sugar and salt, divided between the two jars. Now cover with cold vinegar, leaving head-room of about ¾ in vinegar above onions. Seal tightly and leave for at least 3 weeks or longer if possible.

Method 2. Peel the onions, place them on a flat dish and sprinkle with dry salt. Next day drain off the salt, pack into jars and cover with cold spiced vinegar (with sugar but no salt) leaving ¾ in vinegar above the onions. Into this vinegar pop a little bag (made of muslin or cotton) full of mixed pickling spices, and seal jars securely. Leave untouched for 3 months.

Note: *See the warning on p. 7 regarding proper lids for these pickles.*

38

Spiced Fresh Peaches

This recipe may be used for fresh-picked peaches, dried ones or even the tinned variety.

2 lb peaches
1 lb sugar
½ pint malt or white wine vinegar
¼ oz mixed pickling spices
¼ oz cinnamon stick (or ground cinnamon)
¼ oz cloves

Blanch the peaches by dipping them in very hot water and then remove the skins. Cut them to remove the stones. Crack the stones and take out the kernels.

Tie the spices in a muslin bag; boil the vinegar and sugar and suspend the bag of spices in the mixture by tying it to the saucepan handle. Place the halved peaches in the boiling vinegar and 'poach' them gently by keeping the spicy vinegar at just simmering point. When the peaches are tender remove them carefully and put them straight into hot, sterilised jars. Boil up the pickle again until it is syrupy and thick. Pour it over the peaches. Seal well.

Pickled Tinned Peaches

1 tin peaches, strained
Spiced vinegar
Sugar

Measure the syrup from the tin, and retain. The peaches may now be pickled in two ways:
1. Replace all the syrup with a sweet spice pickle made in the proportion of 1 pint spiced vinegar and 1 lb sugar boiled together until the quantity is reduced to the same as the syrup it is replacing. (The peach syrup may be used to make a pudding.)
or
2. Take half the syrup in the tin and make up the total with spiced sweet pickle in the same proportion as above. Boil until the required quantity and consistency is attained.

When the pickle is ready pour it while still hot over the peaches and immediately seal securely.

Do not keep too long. Ready to eat in a few days.

Quince Pickle

3 lb quinces
1 lb brown sugar
1 stick cinnamon
½ pint vinegar
½ oz cloves

Peel and slice the quinces. Put them into a pan with the vinegar, sugar, cloves and cinnamon; boil together for about 2 hours or until the fruit is tender. Allow to cool, then pour into jars, and cover closely.

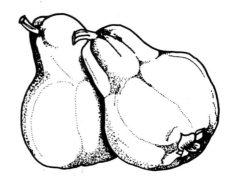

Pickled Red Cabbage

½ large red cabbage or 1 smaller one, firm and of good colour
Salt
Cold spiced vinegar

Shred the cabbage finely, removing any coarse or discoloured leaves. Place the shreds in a large bowl or, if preferred, in a strainer or sieve not made of tin. Sprinkle each layer with salt, and leave for 24 hours.

Drain thoroughly, then pack into suitable jars or bottles but avoid packing too tightly.

Cover with cold spiced vinegar.

Note: *This cabbage is ready after a week, but will lose its crispness after 2–3 months' storage. Stone jars are ideal for this pickle.*

Spiced Rhubarb Pickle

Most country gardens contain a few crowns of rhubarb, but if your garden is not one of these, there are usually those with plenty to spare which they will be glad to find a home for. If not, buy some—it's cheap and cheerful and makes excellent pickle.

Here is an old and tried favourite:

4 lb rhubarb
1 orange
2 lemons
½ pint malt vinegar
3 lb brown sugar (granulated will do)
Allspice
½ oz cloves
1 stick cinnamon

Clean the rhubarb and chop it up into very small pieces. Put it into a pan, add the sugar and vinegar and the juice and grated

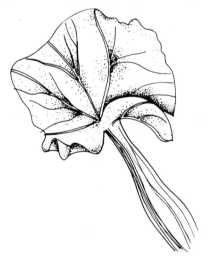

rind of the orange and lemons (remember to grate them before extracting the juice—or put the whole thing in the liquidiser). Tie the spices in a muslin bag, tie it on the handle of the pan and suspend it in the the contents. Heat this gradually and stir until it boils. Skim and stir frequently and continue to boil gently until it thickens. Remove the bag of spices and, when cool, pour the mixture into jars or bottles and cover at once.

Pickled Samphire

Samphire
Salt
Vinegar

Gather the samphire young and green near the end of July, before it flowers. Break into 2 in. lengths, lay on a dish and sprinkle with dry salt. Leave for 24 hours.

Drain, then cook gently until tender in enough vinegar to just cover it, but don't allow it to get soft. Plain vinegar is best for this as the samphire has its own spicy flavour. Seal down securely in hot jars.

Slimmers' Pickle—Uncooked

Since so many of us have to watch our weight these days, here is a welcome addition to your new way of life. Taken with a plateful of salad and a good farmhouse Cheddar cheese, some cold fish or meat, what could be more appetising? If this works for your palate, why not make experiments in other recipes by substituting saccharin tablets or liquid for sugar.

Small cucumbers
1 gallon cider vinegar
3 tbsps mixed spices
1 tbsp powdered alum
2 tbsps dry mustard
1 tsp liquid saccharin (or equivalent tablets)
1 oz salt, or more to taste

Fill some clean baked or boiled jars with small ridge or any cucumbers which you have previously scrubbed and cleaned thoroughly. To make the vinegar mixture, mix the other ingredients together but do **not** heat. Pour the vinegar mixture right over the cucumbers to the tops of the jars and seal securely. Store in a dry dark place if possible.

Spanish Onions, Pickled

Another recipe for slimmers. These are pickled onions with a difference. Use a pretty jar if possible for this recipe and serve with an old-fashioned pickle fork if you have one. For those who find chasing the usual **whole** *pickled onion round a jar frustrating, this is the answer to your prayer.*

A few Spanish onions
Vinegar (malt or spiced)
Salt and cayenne pepper to taste
A little brown sugar—or a few
**   saccharin tablets (or liquid**
**   saccharin)**

Simply slice the onions thinly and lay in the jar, sprinkling with the salt and pepper every now and then. Top up with the sliced onions and make a final sprinkle of salt and pepper. Cover with vinegar in which has been dissolved a little brown sugar to taste, or the equivalent in saccharin. Cover securely and keep in a dry dark place. The pickle will be ready to eat in a month.

Green Tomato Pickle

From Queensland, Australia.

4 lb green tomatoes
2 lb onions, sliced
4 pints vinegar
2 lb golden syrup (or less, to taste)
3 tbsps cloves
2 tbsps mustard seed

Slice the tomatoes, sprinkle with salt between each layer and let them stand for 12 hours. Then drain them well, taking off all the liquor. Add the sliced onions.

Mix all the other ingredients and heat them almost to boiling point, then add the tomatoes and onions and cook for 10 minutes more at a good steady boil, making sure the onions are cooked, and the tomatoes are soft.

Leave to cool, and then bottle closely.

Green Tomato and Orange Relish

1 lb greeny-yellow tomatoes
12 oz granulated sugar
2 oz crystallised ginger (see p. 22)
2 oranges
2 lemons
Mixed spice to taste
3 tbsps white vinegar

Cut the tomatoes into four, cover with sugar and vinegar and leave overnight. Next day add all the other ingredients, including the grated rinds and juices of the citrus fruits. Simmer until the tomatoes are transparent and soft. Spoon them into jars and then boil the syrup until it shows signs of thickening. When the syrup is cool, top up the jars. Seal well.

Pickled Walnuts

Walnuts will stain your hands a lovely woody colour, so the first essential is a pair of rubber gloves—if you care. The walnuts must be gathered while their outsides are green and soft usually in July. Test each one with a silver fork or needle and discard any hard ones.

2 lb walnuts
Brine made of 4 oz salt and 2 pints
  cold water
Spiced vinegar
12 oz sugar (optional)

Cover the walnuts with the brine and leave for at least 3 days. Remove the nuts and dry on a cloth or tray, preferably in the sun, moving them to get as much sun as possible all over. This may take 2 days unless very hot weather prevails.

When they are quite black, pack into jars and cover completely with spiced vinegar. If a sweet spiced vinegar is preferred, add 12 oz sugar to 2 pints spiced vinegar.

Seal securely and do not open for at least 1 month.

Chutneys

*Such and so various are the tastes of
men*
From 'Pleasures of Imagination' by
Mark Akenside, 1721–1770

Chutneys probably originated in India, as our word comes from the Hindustani 'chatni', which is 'a hot Indian condiment of fruits, chillies, etc.' The real chutney is based on mangoes, but we can make a very good version with our own native fruits pepped up with spices, chillies or what you will.

Chutneys may be offered as an addition to a cold help-yourself type meal, or to enhance the simplest or most complicated curry. The blending of the many and various fruits into a spicy condiment is a pleasing, satisfying and surprisingly easy pastime.

Chutney takes a lot of simmering to blend the various fruits, spices and seasonings into a glorious jam-like consistency —though of course it doesn't 'gel' like jam. The smell of cooking can go right through the house, so choose your time and opportunity for cooking until windows may be safely left open since, as has already been hinted, what is a delicious aroma to some is 'What's that horrible smell?' to others.

Unspiced vinegar is generally used for chutneys since one's own individual taste decides the nature of spicing. In this respect it is as well to note that a tried and proven method is to make a small quantity of the chutney recipe that appeals to you, in order to try out the depth of spiciness. Naturally, in reducing the quantity, the ingredients must be reduced pro rata. At this stage you can also decide whether you need more or less salt or sugar. Always remember that the chutney is being made *by you* mostly *for you* and therefore it is *up to you* to choose *your own* spices and flavourings.

Up to a point, chutney-making is pretty foolproof. In a very dry season when the fruit is less juicy, you may have to add a little more vinegar to the chutney. On the other hand, in a wet season when the fruit is juicier than usual, the chutney may seem to be too wet; this can be overcome by simmering carefully to reduce the liquid content. When cooking chutney, always stir at frequent intervals to avoid 'catching'.

Most chutneys improve with keeping, so try and save one jar, at least, from each batch for a later date. Don't forget to make use of your freezer to ease your chutney-making; for example, Runner Bean Chutney, one of the most delicious in the book, may be made on the coldest winter day with temperatures below zero, by using frozen runner beans.

It is a good idea to save any small screw-top jars you may come across, so that you can pop into them that little bit of chutney at the bottom of the saucepan as a present for a lonely or elderly person.

Remember! It pays to label your jars.

Apple Chutney

Apples are such a standby. Here is a recipe which anyone can make very easily and at most times of the year, since all the ingredients are readily available in any area.

3 lb cooking apples
1 lb sugar, brown or granulated
1 oz salt
1½ pints vinegar
8 oz raisins, dates or sultanas
½ tsp cloves
2 oz crystallised ginger (see p. 22)
1 lb tomatoes
1 lb onions
¼ tsp cayenne pepper

Core and peel the apples and cut them up, together with the onions and raisins. Put all the ingredients into a pan and cook gently until the mixture thickens. This takes about 1½ hours. Stir well until the chutney comes to the boil and keep stirring at frequent intervals while the slow cooking is in progress. When the mixture is thickened put it into hot jars. Seal securely at once.

Apple and Blackberry Chutney

1½ lb cooking apples, prepared
½ pint vinegar
8 oz sugar, brown if possible
1 tsp salt
1 tsp cayenne pepper
1 tsp ground ginger
1½ lb blackberries
4 oz stoneless raisins
4 oz sultanas
2 cloves garlic *or*
3 small onions, chopped finely

Put the blackberries in a pan with the vinegar and crush well. Simmer together, then rub through a sieve. Add the remaining ingredients. Stir well and often to dissolve the sugar. Now cook gently at

simmering point until the mixture thickens, still stirring at frequent intervals—this takes about 45 minutes. If using garlic, remove it after cooking. Put the hot chutney into warmed jars and cover down firmly.

Apple and Marrow Chutney

A delicious chutney, easy and cheap to make. Allow extra total time because of the marrow, which being mostly composed of water needs to be brined before being incorporated into the chutney, otherwise the liquids are out of balance with the rest of the ingredients.

3 lb marrow
1½ lb cooking apples
1 lb onions
1 lb sugar
½ oz pickling spice
1 oz black peppercorns
8 oz sultanas
2 pints vinegar
Salt for brining

Prepare the marrow by peeling it and taking out the seeds. Then cut into cubes and put on a flat dish. Sprinkle with salt and leave for 24 hours, then drain well.

Put the marrow into a saucepan and add the apples, sliced thinly, and the onions, chopped up finely. Pour on 1 pint of the vinegar and cook the fruit until tender. Now add all the other ingredients and simmer gently until the chutney thickens up nicely. Pour into hot jars and seal securely at once.

Apricot Chutney

No apologies for including this one. If you have apricots, use fresh; if not, dried will do very well.

1 lb dried apricots
1 onion, chopped
3 oz sultanas
½ pint white vinegar
12 oz sugar, brown or granulated
1 tbsp salt
2 tsps pickling spices

If possible, obtain the large dried apricots and soak in water until soft. Pour off the surplus water, then cook the apricots and chopped onion until tender in a pan with the lid on. Add the other ingredients, putting the spices in the usual muslin bag and suspending it in the mixture. Bring to the boil, stirring constantly, and simmer until the right thickness has been reached. Put in hot jars. Seal securely, and store in a cool, dry, darkish cupboard if possible.

Banana Chutney

A good simple recipe to use, especially if you are on good terms with your grocer or fruiterer and thus have access to cheap over-ripe bananas.

6 bananas
½ pint vinegar
½ oz curry powder
4 oz (brown) sugar
3 oz sultanas
2 good pinches ground cinnamon
1 tbsp salt

Peel the bananas and cut up in a saucepan. Add the vinegar and boil to a pulp. Stir in the sugar until it is all dissolved; set aside to cool. Rough-cut the sultanas and add, with all the other ingredients, to the bananas; leave until cool. Stir all together and stand aside again to soak in for 12 hours. Now bottle up and cover securely.

Beetroot Chutney

Delicious!

1½–2 lb beetroot
8 oz shallots *or* 1 large onion
1 large cooking apple
12 oz sugar
1 tsp salt
½ pint spiced vinegar
½ tsp ground ginger

Boil the beetroot in salted water until tender (the time taken will vary according to size). Skin the beetroot and put it through a fine mincer or chop into cubes. Chop the apples and onions and put them in a saucepan with the vinegar. Add all the other ingredients except the beetroot, and boil for half-an-hour. Add the beetroot and cook gently for a further 15 minutes, stirring very often. Put in hot jars and seal securely at once.

Blackberry Chutney

1 lb cooking apples
3 lb blackberries
6 medium-sized onions
1 pint vinegar
1 lb demerara sugar
1 oz mustard
3 oz salt
1 oz ground ginger
1 tsp ground mace
$\frac{1}{2}$ tsp cayenne pepper

Prepare the apples—there is no need to peel them if you cut them up very finely, but remove the core. Chop the onions and put them in a saucepan with the black-berries (unless you must, please don't

wash them) and chopped apples. Add the vinegar and spices and cook for 1 hour. Add the sugar and cook for a further 2 hours. The chutney may be sieved at this stage if liked. Put into hot jars and seal right away.

Chutney-All-Sorts

A useful chutney to make from small quantities of mixed fruits, etc. 4–5 lb in total.

Apples—one or two of the best of
   the windfalls
Rhubarb—a stick or two
Green tomatoes
Pears
A few late plums or damsons
3–4 average-sized onions
A handful of hazelnuts (if available)
1 tbsp curry powder
10–12 oz sugar
A good tsp salt
Sultanas
Vinegar
1 tbsp hot sauce (optional)

Prepare each ingredient according to its kind. Put all the ingredients except the curry powder, sugar, sauce, salt and sultanas into a large saucepan, and barely cover with vinegar. Cook until all is soft. Now add the sugar, salt and sultanas.

Mix the curry powder with a little cold water and vinegar to make a smooth paste, and mix into the chutney. Bring back to the boil, stirring well. Cook and stir for another 10–15 minutes, or until thick enough; if desired, add the hot sauce just before cooking is finished. Bottle up in small hot jars.

Cover when cold.

Cranberry Chutney

2 quarts cranberries (i.e. measured in a 2-pint jug)
$3\frac{1}{2}$ lb sugar
1 lb chopped raisins or sultanas
8 oz onions, chopped
$\frac{1}{2}$ pint vinegar
2 oranges, juice and rind
$\frac{1}{2}$ oz mustard seed
1 level tsp ground ginger
1 level tsp powdered cloves
1 level tsp cinnamon
Salt and pepper to taste

Pick over the cranberries as necessary. Put them in a saucepan with the other ingredients and boil until thick, stirring frequently.

Bottle in hot jars and seal securely.

Date and Apple Chutney

2 lb cooking dates
2 lb cooking apples
1 large or 2 small onions
8 oz brown sugar
1 pint vinegar
1 tsp salt
1 tsp mustard
1 tsp ground ginger
A pinch of cayenne pepper

Put the apples (peeled and cored), dates and onions through a mincer. Add the spices and vinegar and simmer until tender.

Bottle up in hot jars and seal at once.

Elderberry Chutney

1 lb elderberries
2 oz sugar or
1 good tbsp syrup
1 small onion
$\frac{1}{2}$ pint vinegar
$\frac{1}{2}$ tsp ground mixed spice
$\frac{1}{2}$ tsp ground ginger
A pinch of salt

De-stalk the berries and wash if absolutely necessary (better not to). Mash them well. Put all the ingredients into a saucepan, bring to the boil and cook gently until the chutney is thick, stirring frequently to prevent burning.

Bottle into hot jars while very hot and tie down securely.

Fig Chutney

If you happen to have a flourishing fig tree, this delicious recipe may be made up from some green figs.

1 lb green figs
½ pint vinegar
8 oz onions
1 tsp salt
4 oz brown sugar (white will do)
½ oz black pepper
2 oz crystallised ginger (see p. 22)

Cut up the figs, onions and ginger quite small. Put into a saucepan the vinegar, salt, sugar and pepper. Bring to the boil, then add the figs, etc. Boil up again. Allow to simmer until the mixture thickens nicely. Pour into hot jars and seal at once.

This will not keep too well—but are you likely to want it to?

Gooseberry Chutney

1 lb gooseberries
4 onions
8 oz stoned raisins
1½ lb (brown) sugar
¼ oz mustard seed
2 tbsps salt
½ tsp cayenne pepper
¼ tsp turmeric powder
1½ pints vinegar

Tie the mustard seed in a muslin bag (or similar). Put all the ingredients in a saucepan, bring to the boil and simmer for about 2 hours or until the gooseberries are pulpy. If too thick, add a little more vinegar. Take out the muslin bag, bottle the chutney in hot jars and seal at once.

If you prefer, the chutney may be sieved before bottling.

Hot Indian Chutney

This is intended for hot curry addicts rather than those with a more dainty palate!

1 pint vinegar
2 lb cooking apples
2 lb brown sugar
8 oz stoneless raisins
1 lb sultanas
4 oz salt
1 oz garlic (or onions if preferred)
2 oz mustard seed
1 oz red chillies
1 tsp ground ginger ⎫ **for those who**
1 tsp ground cloves ⎬ **like extra**
1 tsp allspice ⎭ **spiciness**

Peel (optional) and slice the apples and spread on a flat dish. Sprinkle with the salt and leave for 24 hours. Then drain them well and put in a pan with half the vinegar; boil till tender. Stand aside overnight. Now mince the sultanas, raisins, chillies and garlic (or onions) together; pound the mustard seed (failing all else place the seed in a paper bag, then between two thick layers of newspaper crush with a hammer or similar weapon).

Into another saucepan put the sugar and the rest of the vinegar and boil to a syrupy thickness. Add the crushed mustard seed and the ground ginger and simmer gently for another 5 minutes. Now add the minced dried fruits, etc., and last of all the apples in vinegar. Mix really well and simmer until thick. Dish up into hot jars and seal tightly.

This is a good keeper—in fact it improves with age, providing it is securely sealed. Use sparingly—and keep away from children!

Indian Chutney

A milder recipe.

**4–5 lb cooking apples
1 lb onions
1 lb sultanas
1 lb sugar
1 oz salt
1½–2 pints vinegar
1–3 tsps dry mustard
1–3 tsps ground ginger
A few cloves (optional)**

Peel and core the apples and chop them and the onions finely, or put all the first three ingredients through a mincer. Now put all the ingredients into a large saucepan and bring carefully to the boil, stirring frequently. Cook long and gently until the chutney thickens nicely. Add more vinegar if desired. Heat jars and bottle when hot; seal securely.

This chutney is the better if left to mature. It keeps well if the seal is effective.

Lemon Chutney

An unusual chutney but well worth trying.

**3 lemons
8 oz onions
4 oz sultanas or raisins
12 oz (brown) sugar
½ oz cayenne pepper
1 pint vinegar
1 oz salt**

Slice the lemons and remove the pips if you like. Chop the onions, lay them with the lemons on a flat dish and sprinkle with salt. Leave overnight (12–14 hours if possible). Next day, put this all just as it is into a pan with the rest of the ingredients, cook and stir until it boils. Simmer gently for half-an-hour. Pour into hot jars and seal at once.

If preferred, the lemons may be squeezed of their juice and their skins may be minced with the onions. The juice and other ingredients are then added and cooked as above.

Mangold Chutney

**4 lb mangolds
1 lb shallots
12 oz sugar
3 pints spiced vinegar
A small tbsp turmeric**

Peel the mangolds and cut up into suitable pieces to put through the mincer. A bread knife or sharp carving knife may be necessary for the job.

Spread the minced mangold on a flat dish and sprinkle well with salt. Leave overnight or a little longer. Strain well and then add the shallots (minced), sugar and vinegar. Boil together for about 1 hour. When the ingredients are cooked, add the turmeric and bring to the boil again for a moment or two, stirring frequently. Bottle into hot jars and seal very well.

This quantity makes about 8 lb. If reducing quantity, remember to reduce **all** *the ingredients in the same proportions!*

Marrow Chutney

In a good year when everyone seems to have too many marrows, try serving a baked, stuffed marrow (stuffed with minced meat, onions, herbs or curry, breadcrumbs and seasoning) with Marrow Chutney and new potatoes with side-salads or cooked vegetables.

1 large vegetable marrow
1 lb (brown) sugar
8 oz sultanas
$\frac{1}{4}$ oz cayenne pepper
1 pint vinegar

1 clove garlic (or 8 oz onions or
  shallots if preferred)
1 tsp ground ginger
1 tbsp salt

Peel the marrow and remove seeds and pith. Cut up very small. Put into a large saucepan with the sugar and cook-and-stir until all the sugar is dissolved. Stir occasionally and cook until the marrow is tender. Now add the vinegar and other ingredients and, still giving an occasional stir, cook gently until the mixture thickens. Bottle into hot jars and seal securely.

Marrow and Ripe Tomato Chutney

2 lb prepared marrow
2 lb ripe red or yellow tomatoes
8 oz onions
$\frac{1}{2}$ oz salt
$\frac{1}{4}$ tsp paprika
A pinch of cayenne pepper
$\frac{1}{2}$ pint vinegar
12 oz sugar
$\frac{1}{4}$ tsp ground cinnamon
$\frac{1}{4}$ tsp ground allspice
$\frac{1}{4}$ tsp ground mace
$\frac{1}{4}$ tsp ground cloves

Put the tomatoes in a bowl and cover them with boiling water. When cooled sufficiently, remove the tomato skins and sufficiently, remove the skins and hard core. Cut up roughly. Mince the marrow and onions. Put into a saucepan with the tomatoes and cook-and-stir carefully, adding the spices and salt as soon as enough liquid has started to run out of the fruits. Continue cooking very gently for $1\frac{1}{2}$ hours without the lid. Now add the sugar carefully and stir until it has all dissolved. Add the vinegar and simmer the whole mixture until it is thick—about 20 minutes.

Bottle up into hot jars and seal at once.

This should make about 3lb for keeping and a little for tasting!

Mint Chutney

2 teacups sugar
2 teacups vinegar
1½ cups mint leaves pressed down
  lightly
1½ cups seedless raisins or sultanas
8 oz tomatoes, ripe or green
1 lb cooking apples
1 lb onions
2 tsps salt
2 tsps mustard

Using the same cup throughout for measuring, put the vinegar, sugar and salt-and-mustard (previously mixed with a little of the vinegar) into a saucepan and heat. Mince all the other ingredients and add to the vinegar mixture; boil for 20 minutes. When thick enough, bottle up in hot jars and seal securely.

This is a different and interesting little chutney (to use the jargon of wine-makers and drinkers!), delicious with cold meats, and makes a good filling for sandwiches.

Orange Chutney

4 oranges
2 large cooking apples
8 oz sugar
4 oz preserved ginger (see p. 22)

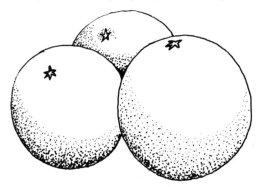

1 large onion
½ oz mixed pickling spice
1 pint malt vinegar
1 tsp salt
A little pepper
2 oz seedless raisins

Peel the oranges and cut into small pieces, removing the pips and pith as you go. Peel, core and chop the apples and chop the onion. Put all these into a pan with the rest of the ingredients, tying the spices into a bag of muslin and suspending it in the chutney from the saucepan handle. Boil slowly, until the fruit is tender—about 1 hour. Remove the bag of spices, and bottle in hot jars; seal securely while hot.

Peach Chutney

Should you be lucky enough to have a peach tree well-laden with fruit, this may appeal to you. You may even feel it is worthwhile in a glut year, when peaches are plentiful, to buy a few and make this unusual luxury. Peach chutney may also be made to advantage with dried peaches or dried apricots, since they have less water and are sweeter than many fruits. Only the method is different.

1 lb peaches
8 oz onions (or 1–2 cloves garlic if
  preferred)
1 tsp ground ginger or preserved
  ginger (see p. 22)
½–1 pint vinegar
8 oz raisins or sultanas
1 tsp cinnamon

Method for Fresh Peaches:

Cut up the fruit, cover in vinegar; put with all the other ingredients into a suitable pan; using the stir-and-boil technique bring gently to the boil until chutney consistency is reached, using a wooden spoon to stir frequently to prevent any danger of 'catching'. Bottle into hot jars and seal at once.

Keep for two weeks before using—if possible. This improves the flavour.

Method for Dried Peaches or Dried Apricots:

Cut up the fruit and pour the whole pint of vinegar over it. Leave to stand for 24 hours. Then proceed as for Fresh Peach Chutney.

Pear Chutney with Oranges

An unusual recipe but well worth trying, especially if you have access to plenty of pears.

3 lb cooking pears
2 oranges
1 onion
1½ lb sugar
1 lb seedless raisins
½ pint vinegar
1 tsp ground cloves
1 tsp mixed spice
1 tsp ground cinnamon

Prepare the pears by peeling them and cutting out the cores. Chop the pears and the onion. Slice the oranges finely and remove the pips and any coarse pith. Put the orange slices and all the other ingredients into a suitable saucepan and bring to the boil, stirring frequently. Reduce to a gentle simmer and, still stirring occasionally, cook for a further 2 hours or until thick enough to bottle. Bottle up in hot jars and seal securely.

Plum Chutney

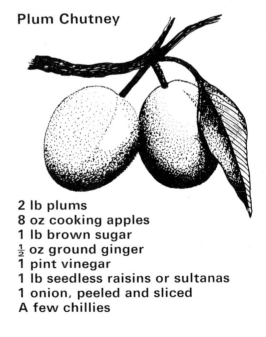

2 lb plums
8 oz cooking apples
1 lb brown sugar
½ oz ground ginger
1 pint vinegar
1 lb seedless raisins or sultanas
1 onion, peeled and sliced
A few chillies

Cut open the plums and take out the stones. Peel, core and slice the apples. Put all the fruit in a suitable pan with the sugar. Cook-and-stir very carefully until the mixture boils. Now add the sultanas or raisins, onions, spices and vinegar. Boil all this together until the fruit is tender and the mixture has thickened.

Fill hot jars with the chutney and seal securely.

Plum and Carrot (or Apple) Chutney

This is a useful recipe as carrots can be substituted for apples if the latter are not available or if there is a glut of carrots.

2 lb prepared plums (i.e. weighed after stoning)
1 lb carrots or apples
8 oz onions *or* **1 large onion** *or* **1 oz chopped garlic**
1 oz ground ginger
1 pint vinegar
$\frac{3}{4}$–1 lb seedless raisins or sultanas
1 lb (brown) sugar
A few chillies

Put the de-stoned plums into a suitable saucepan. Mince the carrots and onions; or chop the apples and onions finely. Put these with the sugar into the saucepan. Cook-and-stir until boiling. Now add the spices, vinegar and dried fruit. Boil all together until the fruit is cooked and tender. Pour into hot jars and seal at once securely.

Quince Chutney

If you do not have a quince tree (and how many of us do not?) try buying them at a Womens' Institute Produce Market Stall or some other country produce shop.

2 lb quinces
1 large onion
8 oz seedless raisins
1 lb brown sugar
1 pint vinegar
$\frac{1}{2}$ oz peppercorns
1 tsp salt
1 tsp mixed spice

Peel, core and slice the quinces. Put the fruit into a suitable saucepan. Add the vinegar, raisins, chopped onion, sugar and spices and boil all together for 2–3 hours or until the quinces become pulpy.

Pour into hot jars and seal securely.

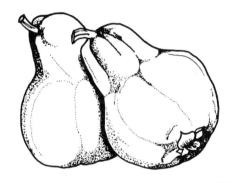

Hot Tip

If your chutney will not thicken even after prolonged cooking, do not despair; just mix a little plain flour with vinegar or cold water and stir into the chutney. Still stirring, boil now for 10 minutes or so to cook the flour.

Quince and Pear Chutney

2 lb quinces
2 lb cooking pears
2 lb onions
2 lb green tomatoes
8 oz sultanas
8 oz seedless raisins
1 lb celery sticks (not coarse)
2½ lb sugar
4 pints vinegar
½ tsp cayenne pepper
½ tsp ground ginger
1 tsp grated horseradish (optional)
8–12 peppercorns
1 tbsp salt

Peel, core and cut up the quinces and pears. Peel the onions. Mince the dried fruit (if liked) and the tomatoes. Put all these in a suitable saucepan with the vinegar and stir-and-cook until the fruits are tender, keeping the lid on between stirrings. Mince the celery and add it, with the sugar, spices, salt and cayenne pepper, to the saucepan. Tie the peppercorns and horseradish (if used) into a bag or square of muslin and tie it onto the saucepan handle, suspending it in the chutney mixture.

Stir until boiling, then simmer gently, stirring frequently, until the chutney is thick—about 3 hours. Remove the muslin bag. Bottle into hot jars and seal securely.

Rhubarb Chutney

3 lb rhubarb
1 lb cooking apples
8 oz onions
8 oz sultanas
1 lb (brown) sugar
1 pint malt vinegar
1 oz curry powder *
1 oz salt
½ tsp cayenne pepper

Some people cannot tolerate curry-flavoured food at any price. For curry powder you can substitute ground ginger, dry mustard, turmeric, or mixed spice, in the same quantity.

Wash the rhubarb and cut it up into small lengths. Peel and chop the onions and apples, or put them through the mincer with the sultanas. Put all the ingredients into a suitable saucepan and heat carefully until boiling, stirring at least until the sugar is dissolved. Simmer for about 2 hours, stirring at frequent intervals. When the mixture is thick, bottle up in hot jars and seal at once, securely.

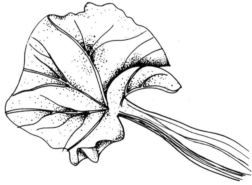

Rhubarb and Date Chutney

1 lb rhubarb
8 oz dark brown sugar
8 oz dates
1 onion
½ pint vinegar
1 tsp cayenne pepper
1 tsp ground ginger
2 tsps salt

Peel the onion and put it and the dates through the mincer. Cut the rhubarb into ½ in. lengths. Cook all the ingredients together slowly in a suitable saucepan, stirring frequently and being in no hurry to boil. When the fruit is soft and the mixture is thick, bottle up in hot jars and seal at once, securely.

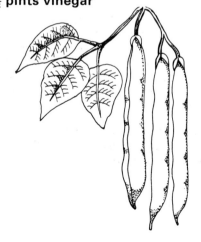

Runner Bean Chutney

An excellent and popular chutney—very easy to make, and useful for those with a row of beans or the odd climbing plant in window box or border. It is even worth buying beans to try this recipe.

**2 lb runner beans, sliced
1 lb (brown) sugar
1½ lb chopped onion
1½ pints vinegar**

Dry Ingredients:
**1 good tbsp dry mustard
1 good tbsp plain flour or cornflour
1 good tbsp curry powder or
   turmeric**

Cook the prepared sliced beans in well-salted water until soft. Mix the dry ingredients with a little of the vinegar and put aside. Cook the onion in some of the vinegar, then add the well-strained beans. Cook for 10 minutes, then add the rest of the ingredients, stirring constantly. Boil for 15 minutes or until thick. Bottle while still hot into warm jars. Seal at once, securely.

Green Tomato Chutney 1

**3 lb green tomatoes
4 large cooking apples
2 small cucumbers (if not available,
   use marrow instead or omit)
3 large onions
6 oz sultanas
12 oz sugar
2 tbsps mustard
Just over 1 pint vinegar
1½ tsps ground ginger
1 level tsp cayenne pepper
1½ tbsps salt**

Peel, slice and prepare the fruits and vegetables, and put them in a large saucepan with all the other ingredients. Bring to the boil. Simmer gently for 2–3 hours, stirring to prevent burning, until quite soft, well blended and thick. Put into hot jars and seal at once.

Best kept for a few weeks or even up to six months to improve the flavour.

Green Tomato Chutney 2

Tomatoes at the end of the season are sometimes so plentiful that even after one has wrapped up pounds of them (as for apples) to ripen for the winter, there is still an abundance. Here is a well-tried recipe which will yield some interesting chutney right now, and more may be made later on if the tomatoes are carefully stored. Store by wrapping each one in a little twist of newspaper, putting in a cool dry place away from frost; or stand in layers with newspaper in between so that they do not touch directly.

1½ lb green tomatoes
12 oz onions
2–3 bananas
1 lb sugar
12 oz sultanas or seedless raisins
1½ pints vinegar (add more if
    needed)
6 oz crystallised ginger (see p. 22)
1 oz salt (or more to taste)
½ tsp cayenne pepper (or more to
    taste)

Chop up the peeled bananas and onions. Cut up the tomatoes, very thinly; or dip in boiling water for a while and remove the skin.

Method 1: Put all the ingredients into a suitable pan and cook-and-stir until thick.

Method 2: Put the tomatoes, fruit and onions into a pan and simmer in the tomato juice, with the lid on the pan, shaking about to prevent 'catching'. Add the rest of the ingredients and simmer, stirring frequently.

Method 3: Cut up the tomatoes, fruit and onions and leave soaking in the pan together until next day. Boil the sugar and vinegar until the sugar is dissolved; add all the other ingredients and stew gently until thick.

Bottle into hot jars when thick and seal securely at once.

Red or Green Tomato Chutney

3 lb tomatoes
1 lb cooking apples or marrow
8 oz onions
8 oz raisins
½ oz salt
1 pint vinegar
1 lb (brown) sugar
¾ oz ground ginger
¼ tsp cayenne pepper
¼ tsp ground cloves

Slice the tomatoes finely and put them in a suitable saucepan. Mince the apples, raisins and onion, or chop finely. Mix all the ingredients in the saucepan and then cook-and-stir for about 1 hour. When all is tender and the consistency thick, bottle into hot jars and seal at once.

Note: *If no marrow or apples are available, just put in extra tomatoes, but add lemon juice or citric acid to taste.*

Turnip Chutney

2 lb turnips
1 lb cooking apples
1 lb onions
8 oz (brown) sugar
8 oz sultanas or seedless raisins
$1\frac{1}{2}$–2 pints malt vinegar
$1\frac{1}{2}$ oz salt
$\frac{1}{4}$ tsp pepper
$\frac{1}{4}$ tsp dry mustard
$\frac{1}{2}$ oz turmeric powder

Prepare the turnips and cook in a little water. Drain well and beat until quite smooth. Prepare the apples and onions and chop up finely. Mix the turmeric and mustard powders with a little of the vinegar. Put all the ingredients into a suitable saucepan and cook-and-stir for 1 hour. When thick, pot up in hot jars and seal securely.

Uncooked Chutneys

Uncooked Apple and Date Chutney

For the busy cook of today, these recipes are invaluable.

Such an easy recipe!

1 lb cooking apples
1 lb cooking dates, stoned
1 lb sultanas
1 lb onions
1 lb (brown) sugar
1 pint vinegar
1 tsp salt
1 bag pickling spices and whole
   ginger
1 pinch each of pepper and cayenne

Mince everything minceable, and put in a large bowl with the bag of spices, vinegar, sugar and peppers. Leave the mixture for 24 hours, stirring every time you think of it, and keeping well covered in between whiles. Bottle up.

This chutney will keep for two years.

Uncooked Apricot Chutney

1 lb dried apricots
1 lb onions
1 lb stoned dates
$1\frac{1}{2}$ lb granulated sugar
$1\frac{1}{4}$ pints white vinegar
1 good tsp cinnamon
1 good tsp salt

Soak the apricots in the vinegar for a few minutes. Prepare and slice the onions, drain the apricots and mince them with the onions and the dates. Put all the ingredients into a large bowl and stir. Stir at intervals until the sugar is melted—this will take about 30 minutes.

Put into jars and leave for one week before tasting.

Uncooked Gooseberry Chutney

1 lb gooseberries
1 lb onions *or* $\frac{1}{4}$ lb shallots
8 oz sultanas or raisins
4 oz sugar
Vinegar
Ground ginger to taste
1 tbsp dry mustard
1 tbsp salt

Prepare the gooseberries by 'topping and tailing' them; peel the onions and mince them with the fruit. Put the onions and fruit in a large bowl and add all the other ingredients. Give a good stir, then cover them with vinegar. Leave to soak for an hour, then bottle up and cover very securely.

This will keep many weeks if kept well covered, but more vinegar may be added— if the chutney looks on the dry side.

Uncooked Mint Chutney

3 tbsps chopped mint
1$\frac{1}{2}$ oz raisins or sultanas
2 tbsps tomato ketchup
1$\frac{1}{2}$ oz dates, chopped
1 tbsp brown sugar
A pinch of salt
A dash of lemon juice or vinegar

When all the prepared ingredients are ready, mix well together, working in the lemon juice and ketchup until the chutney is thick and juicy. Bottle and seal securely, storing in a dry place.

This chutney is a delicious accompaniment to cold lamb.

Ketchups and Sauces

*Cast your bread upon the waters, and
it comes back as buttered toast*
Heard on BBC Radio, 'Thought for
the Day'

Apart from the texture, the ingredients for
ketchups and sauces are the same as for
chutneys, and the initial preparation is the
same; but as you know, ketchups and
sauces have lost their chunkiness so
characteristic of chutneys.

The modern kitchen, with its liquidisers
and blenders, is well equipped for making
this delicious addition to the store cupboard. So often one has a glut of fruit or
mushrooms, and this is the opportunity to
try out one of the following old recipes,
but using the modern mechanical aids
to make the whole operation easy and
pleasurable. Remember, too, that a deep-
freeze makes for simplicity and convenience so that there is no need to start
cooking *now*. For instance, tomatoes and
mushrooms freeze extremely well, as do
nearly all fruit and most vegetables.

If you love making these sorts of things
and have no appreciative audience at
home, now is the chance to indulge in a
pastime which could bring you in a little
pocket money if your products are sold in
local Women's Institute markets or the
type of shop that sells home produce; and
of course, as with all the other pickles and
chutneys, a bottle of ketchup or sauce
makes a useful present-in-the-hand when
calling on a new, an old or a sick neigh-
bour, or to put into the hand of a departing
visitor from your home. It all makes for
goodwill, and be assured—you'll get it
back a hundredfold.

Before you begin, please read Chapter 1
for guidance!

Blackberry Ketchup

5 lb blackberries
*For every pint of juice produced as
instructed below:*
$\frac{1}{2}$ **pint vinegar**
$\frac{1}{2}$ **tsp salt**
1 tsp sugar
$\frac{1}{2}$ **tsp dry mustard powder and a**
  pinch **each of cinnamon, nutmeg
  and ground cloves per 3 pints**

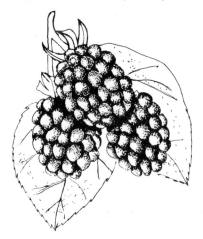

Place the blackberries in a saucepan and
just cover them with water. Simmer until
quite soft (about 25–30 minutes), then
put them through a blender and strain
them through butter muslin (or clean
tights!), pressing out every possible drop
of juice and pulp. This can be done overnight. Measure the juice as you pour it into
a saucepan, and for every pint all the
ingredients listed above—*but don't add
them yet.*

Put the saucepan containing the blackberry juice on a low heat and add the
sugar, salt and nearly all the vinegar.

Gradually add the dry mustard (previously mixed with a little of the vinegar) and the rest of the spices, to suit your taste. When the flavour is right, bring to simmering point and keep it there for 10 minutes.

Pour into heated bottles and seal at once, or allow to cool and then put the sealed bottles in a saucepan of cold water and bring to the boil, taking care to place a folded newspaper in the bottom of the pan to prevent the bottles getting 'bounced' and cracked.

Elderberry Ketchup

Mrs Beeton gives a recipe for 'Pontac Ketchup' which uses anchovies to add to the elderberries. There is no reference to explain how the name 'Pontac' (also used by Mrs Glasse in the 18th century) arose. They cooked their elderberries in the oven, but for most of us saucepans are more economical.

4 lb ripe elderberries
Vinegar

For every pint of liquor produced as instructed below:
A
2–3 shallots (or 1 onion), sliced
$\frac{1}{2}$ tsp powdered mace
$\frac{1}{2}$ tsp peppercorns
1 saltspoon cloves

B
1 level tbsp salt *or*
8 oz anchovies

Place the elderberries in a saucepan and cover them with vinegar. Bring slowly to the boil and simmer for 15 minutes. While still hot, strain off the liquor.

Bring back to the boil and add the ingredients in A. While it is simmering (to cook the shallot) add either salt or anchovies in the proportions listed under B above. The salt is almost as effective as the fish but not quite. Strange, isn't it?

Bottle and seal securely.

Gooseberry Ketchup

This recipe comes from an old friend in Aberdeenshire. She recommends that you should try Gooseberry Ketchup with cold lamb, duck or even pickled herrings!

5 lb gooseberries
$\frac{1}{2}$ pint vinegar
3 lb sugar
1 level tbsp ground cloves
1 level tbsp mixed spice
1 level tbsp cinnamon

Put all the ingredients into a saucepan. Cook slowly, stirring as frequently as you can, for up to 6 hours. Frequent stirring avoids 'catching' the ketchup so dig right to the bottom and right around the edge of the saucepan. Put the mixture through a blender and a sieve if necessary.

Put into wide-mouthed bottles and seal down securely.

Grape Catsup

Many gardeners have planted vines in the last few years. Vines are most accommodating plants to grow because once they have grown their roots—this takes two or three summers as the roots eventually are about 25 feet long—they need very little watering. But if you have no vines, grapes in season are not unreasonably dear and on the principle that if your nearest and dearest were in hospital you would probably buy grapes galore, why not treat yourself to a few pounds in order to try out this unusual recipe?

5 lb ripe grapes
2½ lb sugar
1 pint vinegar
1 tsp cinnamon
1 tsp cloves
1 tsp allspice
1 tsp pepper
½ tsp salt

Boil the grapes in enough water to prevent burning. Strain them in a colander. Put all the ingredients into another saucepan and add the strained grapes. Boil, until a little tested on a cold plate thickens.

Bottle and seal.

Grape Ketchup

This recipe comes from my American daughter-in-law, whose home is in California.

5 lb grapes, preferably the small
 green sweet ones
1 pint vinegar
1 lb sugar
1 tsp ground cloves
1 tsp cinnamon
1 tsp cayenne pepper
1 tsp mixed spice
1 tbsp salt

Put the grapes and vinegar in a saucepan, simmer for about 15 minutes, then pulverise in a liquidiser or press through a fine sieve, or strain and squeeze through clean tights.

Put the resulting pulp back in the saucepan, and to it add the other ingredients. Simmer gently (i.e. just ticking over) until fairly thick, remembering to stir as often as possible. Bottle it up while hot and seal securely. You can allow the ketchup to go cool and then bottle it, but you must sterilise the bottles after filling and sealing by standing them in a pan of cold water on sheets of cardboard or newspaper folded thickly, and bringing them slowly to the boil and allowing it to boil for 15–20 minutes. Leave them in the water until cool enough to handle.

Note: *This is a luxury class ketchup. Don't take this recipe verbatim but try out the spices gradually; don't plonk the whole dose in at one go—you may prefer it less spicy.*

Mushroom Ketchup

The mushrooms must be gathered on a dry day or they will not keep.

3 lb mushrooms
3 tbsps salt
½ oz cloves
½ oz black peppercorns

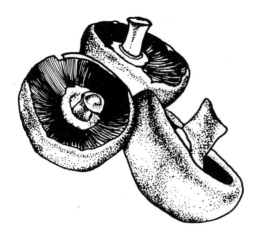

in a suitable pan with the salt and half the vinegar. Boil gently for about half-an-hour until the plums, etc. are soft. Put in blender and/or sieve. Return to the pan, add the sugar, dates and the rest of the vinegar save half a cupful. Bring to the boil.

Now mix the turmeric, ginger and mustard to a paste with the remaining cold vinegar. Stirring all the time, add this spicy mixture to the pan and boil gently together until the mixture is reduced to the consistency of a bottled sauce. Remember it does thicken a little on cooling.

Pour into hot bottles and seal securely.

Cut off the ends of the stalks and wipe the mushrooms carefully. Then break into small pieces, put them in a large jar, sprinkle with salt, cover and leave for three days, strain, then cook in a suitable pan for about 30 minutes; press the contents through a sieve, and allow the liquid to continue dripping all night through. Then put the mushrooms into a saucepan, add the cloves and peppercorns (tied in a muslin bag) and boil for 3 hours.

Allow to cool, remove the bag of cloves and bottle. Screw the tops of jars down very firmly.

Plum Sauce

Very special—from Mary Horrell of Exeter in Devon.

4 lb plums
1 lb onions
8 oz minced dates
8 oz (brown) sugar
2 pints spiced vinegar
2 tsps salt
1 oz ground ginger
$\frac{1}{2}$ oz turmeric
$\frac{1}{2}$ oz dry mustard

Peel the onions and cut into small pieces. Cut up the plums and put with the onions

Sherried Mint Jelly

$\frac{1}{2}$ cup finely chopped mint
1 cup white vinegar
$\frac{1}{2}$ packet lime jelly
$2\frac{1}{2}$ oz sugar
$\frac{1}{2}$ cup sweet sherry
Juice of half a lemon

Use the same cup throughout.

Put the sugar and vinegar into a saucepan and bring slowly to the boil. Simmer for about 3 minutes; remove from the heat, add the jelly, stir until dissolved, then add the mint. Allow to cool a little and finally add the sherry and lemon juice. Mix well.

Pour into small warmed jars with screw tops. When cold, cover with waxed discs and screw the tops down tightly.

Tomato Sauce

1½ lb ripe tomatoes
1½ lb sour apples
8 oz raisins
3 pints vinegar
2 oz whole ginger *or* 2 tsps ground ginger
1 clove garlic *or* 1 large onion

Peel, core and chop the apples, and cook all the ingredients together until well cooked. Put through a blender and/or sieve as necessary.

Pour into hot bottles; seal securely.

A Very Special Sauce

Here is a tasty sauce which will keep for over a year in mint condition. And when you realise the contents you will understand why you must put it out of sight in the wall safe, if not the bank vaults.

2 wineglasses port
2 wineglasses walnut ketchup (see p. 63)
4 wineglasses mushroom ketchup (see p. 61)
1 tbsp cayenne pepper
4 anchovies
2 shallots

Mash the anchovies, then boil all the ingredients together for 30 minutes. When cold, put into sterilised bottles and cork well or seal securely.

Walnut Ketchup

Young green walnuts
Vinegar to cover
1 onion, chopped
Salt
A few cloves
½ tbsp pepper to each 1 pint vinegar

The walnuts must be picked before the shell has hardened—usually not later than the first week in July.

Peel the walnuts and put them in a jar, sprinkle lightly with salt and leave for a week. Stir frequently and keep covered.

Now strain the liquid and pour it into a pan; add the vinegar and boil together. Mash the walnuts (try your potato masher) and pour the vinegar, when boiled, over them. Put into a blender, or press through a sieve; then pour this liquid into a pan, add the chopped onion and the spices, and simmer all together for 30 minutes. Allow to cool, then strain the sauce and pour at once into hot bottles. Cork, and seal securely.

Whortleberry or Cranberry Ketchups

5 lb whortleberries or cranberries
A good pint of vinegar
Up to 2 lb sugar (to taste)
2 oz salt (to taste)
A little clove (if liked)
1 tsp ground allspice
½ tsp ground ginger
½ tsp cinnamon
½ tsp cayenne pepper

These are made in exactly the same way as for Blackberry Ketchup (p. 59) up to the stage where you have strained the 'juice'.

Then, when the juice has been poured back into the saucepan, add the rest of the ingredients.

Bottle hot, as for Blackberry Ketchup, or if cold, sterilise bottlesful of ketchup.

My American daughter-in-law tells me this is a favourite with turkey and other game birds and poultry.

Vinegars

Our Garrick's a salad; for in him we
*   see*
Oil, vinegar, sugar, and saltness agree
From 'Retaliation' by Oliver Goldsmith

These vinegars are included to be used as dressings for salads. The few included may inspire you to try your own. The Americans are very adventurous in their use of herbs and we in these islands have an enormous variety of herbs and suitable ingredients to encourage us to make our own individual experiments.

Cress Vinegar

½ oz cress seed
2 pints vinegar

Bruise the cress seed in a mortar (if possible). Boil the vinegar and allow to cool. Add the crushed seed, cover and allow to infuse for two weeks.
    Strain and bottle.

Cucumber Vinegar

In a glut season, why not try this unusual vinegar to serve with your fish-and-chips or your lobster mayonnaise.

1 pint vinegar
5–6 cucumbers (according to taste)
2 onions (or less, according to
    taste)
2 shallots
1 level tbsp salt
1 tbsp pepper
A dash of cayenne

Peel the cucumbers, slice them into a large bowl and pour on the vinegar. Slice the onions and shallots and add them to the cucumbers with the rest of the ingredients. Let this all stand for five days and then boil it all up together. Allow it to get cold, then strain it through muslin (or tights). Bottle it up and cork tightly. Store in a dark cupboard.

Garlic Vinegar

This is made in the same way as Cress Vinegar using 2 oz finely chopped garlic to every quart of white vinegar.

Mint Vinegar

Pick the mint when it is at its most green and plentiful, strip the leaves from the stalks and pack the leaves into jars. Cover with vinegar.
    Seal the bottles *very* securely and let them stand for two weeks. Then simply strain off the vinegar, bottle it and seal the corks as for wine.

Mixed Herbs Vinegar

In the height of summer when the herbs are at their best, pick a sprig of each one in your garden, such as sweet basil, various flavoured thymes, marjoram, tarragon, etc. Strip the leaves off the herbs and put in a saucepan with 1 pint of water, the juice of a lemon (or equivalent in bottled lemon juice), ¼ pint of vinegar, 4 cloves, 2 shallots (sliced), and if liked, 1 stick of horseradish, grated. Bring this all gently to the boil, keeping the lid on meanwhile to prevent the delicate flavour from escaping.
    Simmer, just ticking over, for 15 minutes, then leave to cool. Strain carefully, and when quite cold, bottle in the usual way, sealing securely and storing in a dark cupboard.

This can be used all the year round, on winter or summer salads, fish or cold meat.

Spiced Vinegar

1 quart malt vinegar
8 peppercorns (black)
$\frac{1}{4}$ oz whole cloves
1 or 2 cloves garlic
1 oz minced shallot
1 bay leaf
1 blade mace
$\frac{1}{4}$ oz allspice
$\frac{1}{4}$ oz cinnamon stick
$\frac{3}{4}$ oz salt

Crush the spices and tie in a small piece of muslin (or old fine tea towel). Place in a jar. Mince and add the shallot and peeled garlic. Add the salt and vinegar. Cover closely. Stand for one week, then place the jar in a saucepan of hot water and bring to simmering point. Simmer for one hour, cool and strain. Bottle and seal securely. Save the spices for further use.

Connoisseurs of spiced vinegar should write to the vinegar companies who may tell you how to make your own very varied spiced vinegar. For best results the vinegar should be spiced way ahead of schedule to have it ready for full flavour.

Pickles and Chutneys
Calendar

This calendar is but a rough guide to the reader. Seasons vary enormously – as for example the shortage of potatoes, 1976; the shortage of apples 1977; the glut of plums 1977 when growers could not afford to pay pickers because of the low price returns. The weather factor – world-wide – has a market effect on fruit and vegetable prices – one country's glut year being another's shortage.

January

Oranges lemons grapefruit grapes bananas cooking apples (from in-store) quinces (from in-store)
(imported) tomatoes
Cauliflower onions carrots celery celeriac mangolds swedes shallots beetroot (from in-store) green cabbage
Raisins sultanas dates prunes figs apples walnuts hazelnuts

February

As for January; end of Seville orange season

March

Everything as for January and February.
Cucumbers
Forced rhubarb towards end of month

April

As above – last of English cooking apples coming onto market from winter store
As above – last of English beetroot coming onto market from winter store
More forced rhubarb coming in
Fresh herbs beginning to appear

May

As above – plus fresh rhubarb early gooseberries very early strawberries
Last of stored cooking apples
Herbs more plentiful

June

As above and now things are really getting interesting
Apricots – fresh imported rhubarb gooseberries strawberries raspberries cherries black currants red and white
Early young carrots spring onions a few cucumbers and courgettes tomatoes
More fresh herbs and the wild ones begin to appear in the country – sorrel and garlic

July

Spanish lemons – may be cheaper – try storing a few in freezer – oranges lemons bananas grapefruit grapes imported apples and now a few early local apples peaches a luxury except in gluts whortleberries should now be ripe in areas where they grow cherries now cheaper rhubarb gooseberries raspberries strawberries blackcurrants tomatoes
Very early apples and plums coming in now
Baby beetroots young marrow and courgettes cucumbers French beans runner beans early carrots young turnips green onions mushrooms shallots in early areas
All herbs – sage mint parsley sweet basil marjoram (wild as well now) garlic
Pickle walnuts while still green

August

Rhubarb coming to end of season in most places
Pear season starts
Apples and plums plentiful especially towards end of month
Some cultivated blackberries
Vegetables plentiful now
Tomatoes should be quite cheap

September

Marrows and purple cabbage
Runner beans
English onions
Some field mushrooms may crop up if rain and sun 'feed' them
'Local' cucumber cheap now

October

Pears and plums
Apples available now
Beans nearly finished
English onions around now but though remember they do not store quite as well as imported ones
Early celery available but its flavour improves after frost
Cucumbers
Red (or purple) cabbage ready now, for pickling
Green tomatoes may be bought from W.I. markets
From the hedgerow, blackberries elderberries crab apples, but leave sloes until the frost has been on them
Beetroot still in season
Damsons ready at end of month
Cauliflower available now
Field mushrooms often plentiful in this month.

November

Cooking apples finishing – surplus being put in store for winter
Few nice blackberries left in hedges but country people say that after September 30th the devil spits on them!
They can be very bitter now
Elderberries few crab apples sloes bullaces sometimes late mushrooms
A few damsons about now if you're lucky enough to find them
Quinces ripe now
Red cabbage green cabbage still cheap
Cauliflowers plentiful
Marrows
Onions
Last of local cucumbers
Shallots swedes turnips available now
Beetroot being 'lifted' for winter storage
Now is the time to gather nuts from hedges. Christmas nuts coming on market any time now

December

Some English Bramley Seedling apples about
A few marrows – now ready for storing
Time to make – Poor Man's Preserved Ginger
Cauliflower – or broccoli – are at their peak now
Local celery coming in now but still plenty of imported about
Imported onions
Few red cabbages may be found

There may be more dates around now and dried figs
Cauliflower still cheap, also green cabbage
Swedes mangolds celery

Index